home comforts

For my mother and father, Lorcan and Frances Lyons

ne comforts

eoin lyons

CURRACH
PRESS

First published in 2008 by

CURRACH PRESS

55A Spruce Avenue, Stillorgan Industrial Park, Blackrock, Co. Dublin

www.currach.ie

1 3 5 4 2

Cover Design by Sin É Design

Origination by Richard Parfrey

Printed in Malta by Gutenberg Press

ISBN: 978-1-85607-971-6

contents

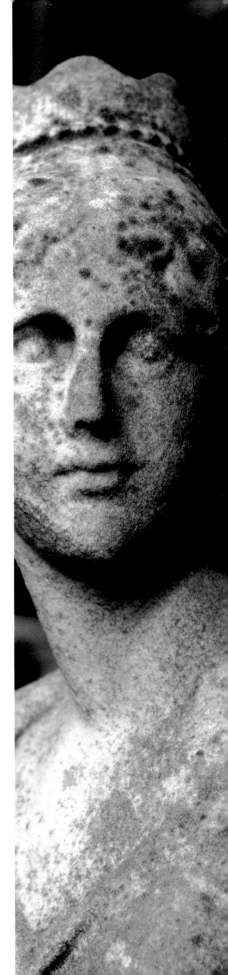

introduction

THERE'S no greater pleasure than loving the way you live. Now more than ever, at a time when we all need a little cheer, it's important to create a home that makes you feel good. Everyone knows that being in a nice environment has a positive effect on one's mood and, while decoration is not terribly important in the greater scheme of things, it can bring a lot of happiness into your life.

This book offers some advice and ideas to those who have limped over the hurdles of looking for, finding, buying or renting a home and are now faced with a space that needs to be organised and made comfortable. For those who have their home a long time, these pages will provide inspiration about how to refresh and improve what they have. Most people at one time or another are faced with renovating and/or decorating at least a room, if not a whole house or apartment. And this is where the difficulties start.

Some people feel that they ought to be able to design their own home but simply cannot get it together; others would prefer to hire an interior designer to take the responsibility off their shoulders but feel they cannot afford one or that it would be self-indulgent (not true). Still others lack time or money or do not know where to find showrooms and shops to see the full choice available.

But decoration is in no way an absolute specialism. It is not like the law or medicine. It is, or should be, highly personal: an expression of self; the sum of your interests as an individual or a family; a personal and practical statement about living. As our lives evolve, so should our homes. Like getting a new haircut, shaking up your wardrobe or getting fit, redecorating is about making a change. Even the smallest update can result in a feeling of renewal.

While I haven't had formal training in the field, my passion for travel and for exploring art and furniture design – along with an architect father – has made design an integral part of my life. I really think that a large part of understanding decoration is about educating your eye. Reading books and magazines on the subject will help you gain confidence and feel at ease with your choice of colour and pattern, scale and texture, furniture and objects.

This book will give inspiration about some of the ingredients available. I use the word ingredients advisedly for, to my mind, decoration is much like cooking: fabrics and papers, floor- and wall-coverings can be chosen and mixed together and spiced and seasoned with accessories in just the same way one experiments with tastes and flavours. In both cases, familiarity with the ingredients is half the battle; interest and the desire to experiment the other.

If this book provides inspirations or any design recipes that help you to achieve what you want, I shall be very pleased. Remember, it's your home: you have to decide what you can live with, live without and really love having around.

Eoin Lyons, November 2008

getting inspired

Opposite: Simplicity is often best, but a white room needs interesting objects to bring it to life. 1950s ceramics and plaster friezes do the job here. The walls, woodwork and cornicing are painted three different shades of white. Mixing more than one shade of white is usually a good idea.

Below: A beautiful rug could inspire a colour scheme.

EVERYONE can create a home that feels good. The trick is to find colours you love and styles of furniture that excite you, and be open to change. Get inspired and be willing to take a few risks. Why not buy that discounted chair you love and figure out later on where it will go?

Decorating your home isn't something you have to do in one fell swoop or with an open cheque book. First decide which changes will make the greatest impact quickly and bring you the most pleasure and which jobs can wait a while. List projects that you can accomplish in a day or a week or a month and those that will take longer.

Look for inspiration everywhere. Buy a few good interior design magazines every month. Tear out pages that inspire. A trip to a museum can throw up expected inspiration: an exhibit of Indian fabrics can spark an idea for a window treatment; even a paint colour or floor finish can inspire. Visit house-and-garden tours of historical properties you might not get into ordinarily. Go to open viewings of interesting houses that are for sale. Pick out what works well and make some of those ideas your own.

Travel educates the eye and beautiful (but not necessarily expensive) hotels can provide great inspiration. Notice how colours or styles of furniture are combined. Also note what doesn't work. Try to analyse what makes a bedroom feel good. Is it lighting, a padded headboard or a restful wall colour?

There are also places to go for inspiration that aren't so literal. Rent a movie or go to the theatre in search of beautiful stage sets. Is there a novel with a mood you'd like to create? Norman Mailer's *The Deer Park* captures the colourful, wacky style of Palm Springs in the 1950s. There's a lot to be said for some decorative fun. Keep a notebook by your bed and write

down late-night or early-morning inspiration. Close your eyes and imagine your dream home. This isn't about thinking of endless rooms with lavish furniture, but an approach on the level of feeling and intuition.

ask yourself:

- Do your ideas fit with the way you live?

- What kind of surroundings make you feel good? Is it a simple space with a few carefully selected items or a room filled comfy chairs and a lot of accessories?

- Do you like things to be neat and organised or do you prefer a room with plenty of stimulation?

- Which is your favourite room in your own home? Which is your least favourite? Think about why.

- Where do you feel most at ease: city or country? Perhaps you could recreate some of the country in the city, or vice versa.

- How much time and money are you willing to spend on particular aspects of your home?

- If you could change one thing about your home what would it be?

- Do you have a favourite piece of art or furniture that could be a starting point for making changes in your home?

- Where would you take your dream holiday? Maybe some aspect of that place can be recreated in your home.

- Is it possible that you do not need a formal dining room if you always entertain in the kitchen?

There are now very many great interior sources around the country, from mass-market to speciality shops, so shop around. Mixing things from inexpensive chain stores and small expensive shops is the way to go. Don't overlook charity shops: you never know what you'll find. If you are buying a large piece of furniture, measure its dimensions when in the shop and recreate the size at home using newspapers. It will give you an idea of how the piece will fit into your room.

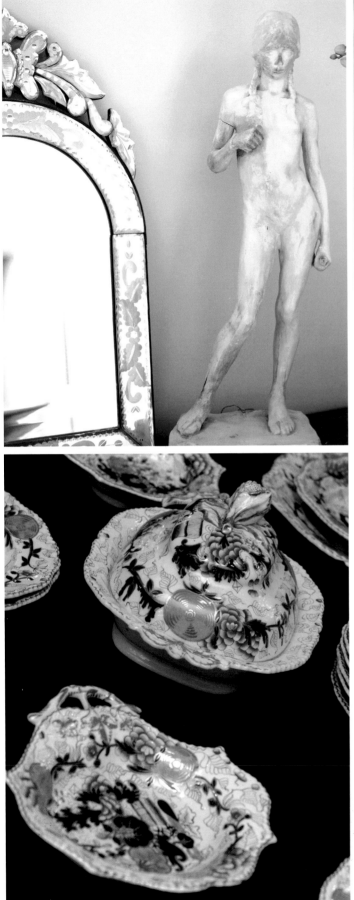

Above left: A Venetian-style mirror and an Italian plaster collectable are the kind of disparate objects that sit well together.

Above right: Inspiration can be found everywhere: the shades of colour in a set of china might work on walls or a floor.

Left: Look to the past for great colour combinations, such as this antique dinner-service.

Small informal arrangements of flowers are effective on any surface.

create a style file

Design ideas can be found almost anywhere. The colour of a dress might spark an idea for a wall colour while a piece of ceramic might be just the look you want to create on a floor.

Carry a digital camera and take pictures of rooms, colours, fabrics and furniture you like. Trust your gut reactions. Tape pieces of fabrics and paint cards you come across into your notebook. Write down the details of shops or sources you come across. This is information you can come back to again and again. Ask friends whom they use as a painter or gardener or whatever. Write down the details so that when time comes you have a ready-to-go list of tradespeople.

Use this notebook to focus your thoughts. Think about how you want to feel in your house: calm, sophisticated, casual or romantic?

Think too about what you *don't* like: maybe you dislike dark spaces or floral fabrics? Or does too much furniture make you feel claustrophobic?

bring nature indoors

Bringing the outdoors inside is one of the easiest and most affordable ways to dress a room. Natural accessories can really change the atmosphere. A simple vase of flowers or a basket of roughly chopped logs makes a room so much more cheerful.

Collect natural memories. From holidays bring back shells, rocks, pinecones – anything that will act as a reminder of your travels. An old piece of wood can be used as a dining-table centrepiece; stones placed in jars in a bathroom; shells used to separate objects on a bookcase.

Bringing nature indoors doesn't necessarily mean spending a lot in a florist's. Greenery from the garden, bunched together in a clear glass container, has a great sculptural quality. Braches or sticks tied together in a vase can look good too. Always keep things unpretentious and stay away from contrived bouquets. Place a single flower beside the kitchen sink or use a row of potted plants on a mantelpiece. Ivy is great in winter – use great big swathes of it tumbling out of a vase.

Big floral statements are wonderful but small arrangements can be effective too. Flowers trimmed short and placed in a cup or wildflowers in a humble jam jar are always beautiful. Use small displays for a splash of colour.

luxury for less

You can make your home special without spending a fortune. Small luxuries offer big dividends. Good-quality sheets, goose-down pillows and fine soaps won't hide that worn carpet or the wall that needs to be painted, but they will make you feel pampered. Small things matter. Wait for the sales and buy the best you can, one good item at a time.

Scented candles and tea-lights should be an everyday treat. Light them when you come home. Buy flowers once a week, even if it's just a single stem or a single piece of greenery. Keep bowls of fruit about the place: apples, oranges or lemons. Even ordinary fruit gives a room a nice atmosphere.

Art always enhances your home. From treasured items such as children's artwork or family photograph to pages taken from an art book, have beautiful things on your walls. Frames are all-important. Chain stores do decent simple ones cheaply but auction rooms often have old (but not particularly valuable) frames that can be picked up for relatively little.

Decluttering will make a big impact. Apart from a bottle or two of Cif, this approach is cost-free. Set aside a weekend to do things such as vacuuming the top of curtains, washing light fittings, shampooing carpets, wiping paintwork and so on. Rope in a few friends – you can always repay them with a good dinner at the end of a day's work. Get rid of as much old paraphernalia as possible. Rooms will look bigger and brighter. Decluttering does not mean living in a super-minimal way and is as much about organisation as anything else. In general, get rid of anything you

Everyone opens their wardrobe doors and wonders where to start decluttering. Have a bag beside your wardrobe and tackle one item per week – for example, shoes, shirts, ties or handbags. At the end of a month, the bag will be full and you will have a tidier wardrobe. Toys create the worst clutter of all. Fill a bin-liner or two with toys, hide them away and if there's no screaming after two weeks, drive as fast as you can to your local charity shop. Always have two bags to fill with things you don't use any more – one for recycling and the other for the charity shop. When the bags are full, move them out of the house straight away; don't leave them sitting by the front door for weeks. Have a charity box in one or two main rooms. It should be deep and have a lid. And it should be attractive. Put a few disposable bags in each box and (over time) as you're cleaning and tidying each room, throw in things that aren't used or wanted any more. Then, when the bags are full, simply lift them out and bring them to a charity shop.

Above left: A plaster relief can lend dimension to a wall.

Above right: A collection of small whimsical pieces, including African wood carvings and a distorted teacup, makes for an interesting display.

Left: Small luxuries go a long way: a fine-quality throw in beautiful colours will make an average sofa seem a bit more plush.

haven't used in the past six months. A home can have only so much broken crockery, odd cutlery and old appliances – all these should go.

Think about the way you display things. Perhaps the hearth of a fireplace could be used to hold a collection of simple glass jars and vases. Everyday objects can be beautiful if grouped together.

discover your look

Spending a lot of money isn't always necessary to make your home feel better. Small luxuries can have a big impact to how the place feels. Experiment – making mistakes with purchases is often the only way to find out what you really like. You can always sell something on or give it away. I'm talking here about inexpensive items, not a table with a four-figure price-tag.

remember:

- One authentic antique is better than a house full of reproductions.

- Mix high and low, old and new, to keep things interesting.

- Keep information in a notebook – paint references, measurements and inspirations.

- Start going to auctions: they're fun and good value.

- Diversify your shopping – department stores, low-end, charity shops – to take advantage of the best each has to offer.

- If you see something you love (and can afford it without going into debt), buy it – you can always work it into your home somehow.

- Look everywhere for inspiration and then make it your own.

Antiques Action

Visit antique shops and auction rooms for one-of-a-kind furniture. Get to know the dealers and ask (nicely) for the opportunity to see how a serendipitous discovery will look and fit in your home before you purchase. Auction rooms won't allow you do this, of course, but shops *will* once you build a relationship with the owner. Everyone knows how well a few pieces of antique furniture can look alongside contemporary furniture. Mixing antiques shows personality. It's not about getting the look (or else reproductions would rule) but about the age and patina of a piece of furniture that's got history. Pieces that are not over-restored are always best – otherwise what's the point? Haggle a little with the dealers but don't go overboard – most reputable dealers are not trying to rip you off and have furniture that is priced according to the market.

colour

COLOUR makes a room sing. That doesn't necessarily mean walls in day-glo shades. Personally I think walls (and curtains) should be relatively neutral, whether dark or light in colour, to allow interesting furniture, art and objects to take centre-stage. Furniture and accessories can provide colour.

ask yourself:

*   What is your favourite colour? Think about what shades you're drawn to most. If you are unsure, flick through a paint colour chart and see what attracts you.

*   How do particular colours make you feel? Do warm colours make you feel comforted and do cool colours calm you down?

*   What's in your wardrobe? Do you reach for neutrals or go for that blue sweater every time? If you feel comfortable wearing a particular colour, you'll probably feel comfortable living with a shade of this colour.

*   Do you want to make a room seem airy or intimate?

*   Do you want all the rooms in your home to be linked by colour or would you prefer to create a different atmosphere in each?

*   Can you live with the colours you already have or do you want a total change?

*   How much daylight does the room get?

Above: Change your accessories (and alter the colours of a room) with the seasons. Cosy wool throws can give way to lighter linen versions in the summer.

Opposite: Pale-green walls in this house in Kerry provide soft colour in a bedroom.

Above left: Balance intense colour with neutrals or white. Monique McQuaid, a chef, has used brightly-coloured upholstered furniture in her living room but kept the walls white and the windows curtainless.

Above right It's safer to introduce colour through occasional furniture: strongly-patterned fabrics work on single armchairs.

Right: In this house in Blackrock, County Dublin, the walls are neutral while the curtains, sofas and artwork add colour.

Opposite: Retailer Sarah Gill on her pink chaise.

choosing colour

Colour affects mood but can also (metaphorically speaking) change the physical space of a room. Painting your walls is the most inexpensive way to make a change in your home. Don't worry too much about mistakes. You can always repaint.

When choosing a paint colour, the only way to do it is to paint a large 4'x8' board with a sample of the shade you're considering. Live with it for a few days and see how you feel. Colour changes depending on the light, so note how it looks at different times of the day. The same goes for all potential furnishing purchases: the blue chair that looked bright in a shop could look closer to navy when you get it home.

Most paints come in many finishes. For woodwork and mouldings, semi-gloss is often best as it gives a nice rich look. Acrylic is easiest to work with and withstands chips.

Matt finishes are best for older walls with imperfections. They're not as good for a bathroom or kitchen as they're harder to wipe down. For those rooms or for children's rooms, try an eggshell finish (it can be washed) or a stain finish (it can be scrubbed).

To make a small space seem larger, white is the obvious option. There are hundreds of variations of white but in general, go for a warm white rather than anything too stark. Soft colours such as pale grey, ivory or light blue can be used as an alternative to white or in conjunction with white: for example you could paint mouldings and woodwork in one of these shades.

In a large space, deep, rich colours can be very successful. They bring the walls closer together and can make a cavernous room more liveable-in. Warm, dark colours can also work in small spaces because they make the room more intimate, if intimacy is what you want to achieve. Vibrant wallpaper is also an option in a large space.

If you can get a professional to do your painting, it's worth it in the long run. (See the Resources section at the end of the book for some recommendations.) If you choose to paint yourself, use quality materials – paint, brushes and rollers. They will help you to get the job done faster and give a better finish. Buying cheap paint is a false economy. It won't give good coverage and could look patchy. A bad brush makes applying the paint much more laborious. Prep your walls and woodwork before you start. That means washing them down, filling in any holes and sanding so you have a smooth surface. Make sure you remove the dust created by sanding. Tape over light switches and remove fittings, if possible, before applying a coat of primer. Paint the ceiling first and then start at the top of the walls and work down. Allow the paint to dry between coats and apply at least two top coats.

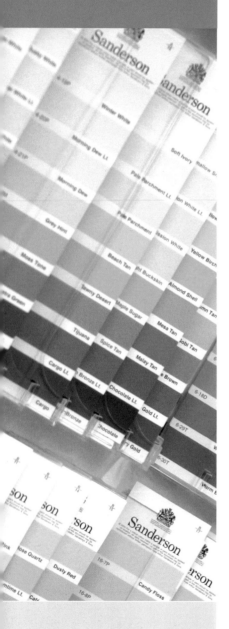

Opposite: It's easier to be adventurous with wall-colour in secondary rooms, such as a games room.

It's probably best to paint rooms that flow into one another (or are closely linked) in the same colour or a slight variation on the colour for the sake of continuity.

other colour thoughts

A patterned cushion is a lot less risky (and a lot less permanent) than a pair of armchairs in the same fabric. Think about keeping major pieces of upholstered furniture neutral. Sofas are expensive and you'll want yours to stick around for many years. Paint, on the other hand, is cheap and cheerful and can create an instant rich result.

Unify your fabric and paint choices. Collect all the pieces of the puzzle on a storyboard to see if you like the mix before ordering anything. When in doubt, men's suiting colours such as camel, navy, grey and white are reliable choices for any fabric element.

It almost always works to use at least four colours in a scheme. Never use just one shade top to bottom. The four colours need not be radically different: you might paint a moulding in a deeper or lighter shade of your wall colour or, on the other hand, use a rug that contrasts with the sofa.

Keeping a rotation of plants and fresh flowers brings ever-changing accent colour into a room.

Feature walls are passé but subtly aged or washed paint effects can be wonderful in almost any setting. Wallpaper brings colour too, but patterns can be too much of a long-term commitment.

dark colours

A black interior is enveloping: done correctly it can be comforting rather than depressing. A few years ago high-end Italian furniture companies put forward interior looks based around the idea of shades of black against black: a black sofa sat on a black carpet with perhaps a black bookcase behind it. It's slick, shiny and seductive. Black might sound oppressive to live with but the trick is balancing it with white and grey, plus shots of

bright colour such as orange and green. Using furniture with high-shine surfaces and textured materials also helps. Layering black is interesting (and brave). But it needs correct lighting – nothing too stark. It's generally good to use black in spaces that do not receive too much direct sunlight. When black is used with a combination of fluorescent and incandescent lighting, the atmosphere can become very luxurious.

white

Call it ivory, oyster, chalk or ecru: white is the right stuff for decorating your home. White is the perfect canvas for beautiful objects and it's also a satisfying colour in itself. White is hot. Paint companies now have whole ranges devoted to different variations of white. Using more than one shade is the key to creating an effect that's neither austere nor clinical.

Why choose white? It's about creating a sanctuary. White is pure and lets you see what's important in a room. It's about clear 'head space' as much as a decorating trend. Life is chaotic. A white room is a place to relax and calm down. Cool, calm and clean, sharp and dynamic, restful or stimulating – the atmosphere you choose is a matter of selecting a palette of white for walls, then mixing in other furnishings for blasts of colour.

A white interior isn't just about white. The successful use of white relies on differences in texture – dark wood, blond oak, woven sisal, white linen, an oriental rug – to give character. The simple beauty of these objects stands out against a white backdrop. Any white room needs accents of colour – small punctuations rather than vast blocks. They are the supporting act, defining the original colour, highlighting it and giving it additional interest, and it is for you to decide whether those accents should be contrasting or toning.

Lighting is important in an all-white room. It is best to control the light with direction-focused lamps. Choose warm whites rather than cool whites, which are more difficult to handle. Cool whites shouldn't be confused with the once-ubiquitous brilliant whites. These shades are responsible for

The living room is this Georgian house is dramatic and glamorous, with a dark parquet floor and glossy furniture. It's the kind of decoration that works best in the evening. It's a night-time room and looks great in candlelight, according to owner Helen Kilmartin. A hang-out space in the evening, it has the feeling of a private club. The walls are painted chocolate brown and the window and skirting are matt black. In the alcoves on each side of the window, panels of striped fabric have been hung. They give the room a little more depth. The chimney breast, covered in silvery wallpaper, relieves all the dark colours. This room is not black at all, although it looks so dark: there are also shades of brown, grey and very dark green.

Interior designer Paul Austen lives in Drumcondra and has decorated his house in various shades of soft white. The result isn't cold but enveloping and calm. Using the house's Edwardian details as a starting point, different shades of white were chosen forthe ceiling, walls and architraves. The walls and woodwork are painted in Farrow & Ball's 'Pointing' and the band above the picture rail is 'Great White', which is actually a very light purple colour. The ceiling is 'White Tie', also by Farrow & Ball. A sheet of mirror hangs on the chimney breast, flush to the wall and unframed so that it opens up the room. At the windows, simple shutters are used instead of curtains. White acts as a backdrop for interesting objects the Paul has collected, such as ceramics from the 1950s. Red tables add bursts of colour and the stained-glass window also provides colour that changes throughout the day. The sofa and armchairs have linen slipcovers that are warm in winter and cool in summer.

Right: Consider lamps as sculpture. The shape of a lamp can become an important feature. Here a gold-leaf lamp that shoe-designer Olivia Morris found in an antique shop brings some fun to her living room.

Opposite above: Chandeliers can work in many different kinds of rooms, bringing contrast to a modern setting.

Opposite below: A 1970s ceiling light used with 19th-century ceiling rose proves that decorating success is in the mix.

any bad preconceptions one might have about white – they have optical brighteners added and lack any subtlety. Cool whites have a dash of blue or black pigment, while warm whites have ochre or pinks. Warm whites take away the clinical look but because most rooms have a different quality of light different shades of white are needed.

The great virtue of white is obvious: rooms seem larger. The downside is also clear: on furniture, it can be hard to keep clean and it's not a suitable colour for rooms used by young children. Have upholstery treated to protect against stains.

It can be argued that white works better in sunnier climates, yet Scand-inavians have long created interiors based around white as a means of reflecting light into the home. White is popular in bedrooms and it's no wonder: it symbolises peace and calm, just what you want in a bedroom most of the time. Again, choose creamy, warm whites – for example, look for any fabric or paint-colour reference that says parchment or buttermilk.

lighting

If you are carrying out a major renovation, lighting should be a priority. Roughly plan where your furniture will be and plan lighting around that. One light source in a room can't serve all your needs. There are four obvious options for fixtures – floor, ceiling, wall and table. With your architect or interior designer, figure out where sockets and switches are needed on the floor plan. For floor lamps, consider fitting sockets in the floor itself to reduce the length of flex needed.

Whatever else you do, use a qualified electrician for anything more complicated that changing a plug. Never attempt electrical work yourself.

Before you buy a light fitting, think about what it must do: is its purpose ambient, accent or task? Ambient lighting creates atmosphere; accent illuminates individual objects such as sculptures or paintings; and task

Look to your wardrobe for colour inspiration. Rails of black clothes don't necessarily mean you want to live in a home full of dark shades but it might signify that you like neutral colours. Accessories are important to an outfit and the same applies to the home. Lamps, rugs, cushions and so on are all easily changeable. Do you have bright clothes you wear again and again? Is green your colour? Match the colour of a favourite item of clothing to a paint chart and try to incorporate it into your home.

Right: This house in Greystones has the palest yellow walls. This is a tricky shade but one that works when paired with complementary shades in furniture and carpets.

Below left: Paint the insides of bookcases or glass-fronted cabinets in a contrasting shade.

Below right: The number of paint ranges available is mind-boggling. Paint large boards with colour samples to get an idea of how a colour will work in your room.

lighting is used to perform a function such as reading, washing up or sewing.

We can't all gut a 19th-century terraced house and pretend it's a modern loft, so experiment and mix styles of light fixtures that don't necessarily 'fit' with the style of your home. Contrast is good. Modern lights look good in a traditional setting and older lights add character to modern apartments. A classic chandelier in a contemporary room makes a great statement.

Table- and floor-lamps can be used to define an area. In large rooms, for example, where one end is for seating and the other for dining, space can be separated visually by means of the old trick of placing a pair of lamps on a table behind a sofa.

Dimmer switches should be fitted not just in living rooms but in bedrooms, kitchens and bathrooms (bright for applying make-up or for shaving, dimmed for relaxing baths in the evening). In a bathroom, make sure your mirror has a light on both sides to provide even light to the face.

Light can be used to direct the eye around a room. Spotlights can focus on a feature or guide the eye upwards. Lights recessed into the floor of a corridor or on a staircase guide your feet and create a nice low-key atmosphere.

It's not good to have light falling straight down in a small room, so install spot-lighting that can be directed in different ways to cast pools of light on the walls. If you light up corners, it draws the eye out to the edges of the room, making it seem larger.

The easiest way to alter the mood of a room is use a low wattage bulb. Glare can also be reduced by using a silver-crowned bulb. The result will be soft light that makes for an intimate feeling.

Always plan the kitchen lighting before having new units installed. The fittings themselves should not be attached until the very end of the decorating process when everything else has been finished.

Make sure that lighting for work surfaces is adequate. Light as many surfaces as you can in the kitchen in order to give maximum flexibility.

Fit dimmer switches to as many lights as is practically possible (remember that halogen lights need to have special inductive dimmers).

Fit a light just outside the back door for reaching the dustbin and for picking outdoor herbs more easily when it is dark. You will also be able to put away any outdoor toys your children leave behind without falling over them first.

If you are using table lamps in the kitchen be careful to avoid leaving trailing flexes where people could trip over them.

Opposite: Parquet flooring can be expensive to lay but creates a lovely feeling in a hall. Hardwoods are also soft underfoot and hard-wearing. This entrance hall has been kept neutral – one way to go about decorating what is essentially a pass-through space – but has enough original features to carry off this approach.

Below: A porch painted pale blue.

entrance halls

THE ENTRANCE HALL is the introduction to the rest of your home, a buffer between you and the outside world. Most people put decorating other parts of the house before their hall. It is nevertheless the first part of your home that you and your visitors step into and the last part that you leave. The way visitors see your home is coloured by that vital first impression made as the door is opened. A warm, welcoming, pleasant hall is good to come home to, less depressing after a hard day than opening the hall door to a dark dull space strewn with schoolbags, sports equipment and shoes. Obviously when you budget the cost of redecorating your home, you have to allow most money for the rooms you are actually going to live in, but once you have decided on that, it's time to turn your thought and care – if not a little money – to making your hall as warm, welcoming and practical as you can. It might come last on your list of necessities but there's no need for it to look the least cared-for.

Theoretically, halls should be easy to design as there is little to purchase in the way of furniture, unless you are blessed with a wide and spacious area. But whatever the size of your hall, you will need to plan for convenience as well as impact, wear as well as warmth.

ask yourself:

- What's the first impression you want to create?

- Is there room to have some built-in storage for coats and bags specially made so the hall doesn't turn into a dumping ground?

- If you live in an apartment, could you use paint colour as a way to mark the difference between the featureless communal corridor and your home?

- Does your hall run through to the living room? Could you use the same flooring material for a unified look?

- Most hallways have several doors: are all your handles matching?

necessities

There should be at least one chair and a table to take all the paraphernalia that will inevitably accumulate. If your hall is too narrow for this – and many entrance ways are barely more than a corridor – try to fit in a long bench or a slender console table, or at the very least have a long shelf attached to the wall and painted to match. If you have built-in cupboards you are home and dry as far as storage is concerned. If you don't, perhaps it is possible to have some storage units made to fit the space, to hold coats, hats and so on. If there really is no room at all, don't use a coatstand or hooks. Put coats somewhere else. Mirrors are unfailingly useful in halls so that you can check your own appearance before going out, while visitors can check theirs coming in. They are also useful for reflecting too small a space and exaggerating very last bit of light. The best place to position them is over the table or shelf.

durability

The materials you choose for your entrance hall should be as tough and durable as you can find. People coming in from outside will bring in dirt and dust and damp so it's a good idea to have both an outer and inner doormat. The most practical solution is to have a slight well let into the floor just inside the front door and to fill it with matting. This way the mat will not shift or slip, will not get frayed around the edges and will not be bypassed. The rest of the floor should be easy to clean.

Country halls look well in materials such as quarry tiles, flagstones, slate or brick. If you are laying these from scratch, lay lunder-floor heating. It should be easy for your builder to do and makes a world of difference. If for some reason you cannot have any natural material, keep your bare boards sanded and sealed. Paint the boards with special hard-wearing paint if they are in bad condition and you cannot afford to lay a new wood floor.

Opposite: The long strips of timber that make up the entrance door of this house in County Wicklow designed by ODOS Architects were painted striking shades of grey, white and black to match the external panels treated the same way.

Below: Interior designer Grania Murray decorated the hallway of this house in Dublin 4. A hallway is often a good space in which to use textured wallpaper: it can give the space warmth and depth. An antique ceiling light fitting works with more contemporary lamps and varies the light available. When using carpet in a hall, it's a good idea to install a mat well at the door. Often these mat wells are allowed to run wall to wall, but in this house Murray created a neat panel in front of the door.

Carpet works in apartments or houses that definitely won't get much wear and tear. Even so, buy the best-quality carpet you can afford. Add rugs to hard floors for softness and interest but make sure they will not slip and cause accidents. Secure them with the slightly sticky weave that is sold to keep rugs in place.

Paintwork in hallways is at constant risk of getting scratched or marked, so finishes must be durable. It's essential to choose paints that can be wiped clean. Nowadays that doesn't mean sacrificing a nice matt finish.

decoration

Ideally, walls on halls, corridors and staircases (if any) should be painted the same colour throughout, unless they are in quite different parts of the house and one section cannot be seen one from the other. Whatever colour you choose for the hall, make sure it leads naturally into the rooms leading off it. Halls tend to to be dark so either choose a pale paint shade (and add colour through furnishings) or, if you want to create something dark and enveloping, make sure the hall is very well artificially lit. Quite apart from the mirror, the hall, corridor and staircase are the perfect places to hang pictures and photographs. If there is space, you could line the walls with bookcases to enormous effect.

lighting

The first essential is a two-way switch so that lighting can be turned on as you come into the hall and off as you enter the living room. Lighting in halls, corridors and staircases should be clear and bright for reasons of safety. But it's also important to be able to vary the lighting at night. Use dimmer switches and have a lamp (or two) on your console table if possible. Downlights – recessed, semi-recessed or ceiling mounted – are good-looking and functional no matter what your style of furnishing. If you do not have many electrical sockets, or cannot add extra recessed spotlights for whatever reason, think of adding track lighting to the ceiling as you can fit many spots on to a track and train them at different angles. If you have a lot of pictures on the walls, this will light them beautifully as well as providing all the light you need. Very dark halls with little natural

Above: Decorative wallpapers often work best in a hallway. Think about coordinating the wallpaper and the floor: here a silvery-green paper complements the stone floor. The main piece of furniture in your hall should be a console table – choose one that's as narrow as possible but wide enough to hold a lamp.

Left: A narrow corridor is often the place to install sliding doors to save on space and cumbersome door-spans. These sliders have opaque glass panels to let light into the adjacent rooms.

light will benefit from strip-lighting recessed behind a pelmet of some kind – a piece of wood, plasterboard or moulding running under the cornice, if there is one, or ceiling angle if there is not. In this way you can achieve lighting without a visible source. Light washes down the walls: a lovely effect.

playing with walls

It has become fashionable to knock the hall and adjacent living room into one, an uncomfortable idea as visitors, welcome or not, step straight in from the street. From a security point of view, getting rid of the buffer between the living area and the street is unwise. But if you are desperate for living space and incorporating the hall would provide it, you could try playing around a little with the walls. For example, in a narrow terrace house where the front door opens directly into a corridor-like space, it might be possible (depending on whether the wall is load-bearing) to take down part of the wall, leaving a little section near the door to offer immediate privacy. Or you could make an arch going into the living room, or lower the wall to seating level so that you get all the benefit of the extra light and space but still have the suggestion of a division. Another possibility, say in an apartment where the living-room door opens off the hall, is to cut two narrow floor-to-ceiling slits in the wall to give both extra light and interesting glimpses of the room ahead.

windows

Look carefully at any windows in your hallway and decide whether you should curtain them, blind them, shutter them or leave them alone. In general, unless you have very long and gracious windows, I think such windows look neater and let in more daylight if fabric blinds are used, simply for practicality – that is, if privacy is an issue. Very small windows are usually better just left. It can be very cosy to curtain the entire wall that holds the entrance door with a thick curtain. Often there are windows around such a doorway so the benefits will be twofold. Hook this curtain to the wall during the day with a decorative tieback.

Dress windows in a hall simply and make the most of the natural light available. Just because a room is small doesn't mean it has to be dark.

Make a painting, a mirror or a fantastic light-fixture the focal point of the space.

Be brave with colour: sometimes a bold monochromatic statement can do big things for a small space.

Search for stylish options to house everything you don't want to see all the time. A handsome chest of drawers or a sideboard can also work in a hall.

Keep the floor as uncluttered as possible. Perhaps use a rug to unify the space.

staircases

Although it may be tempting to think of reinventing your staircase with a sweeping *Gone With The Wind* style model or a modern open-plan design, the end result is usually not worth the cost. Replacement is really only worthwhile if the old staircase is beyond repair. It's easy to modernise the banisters if they're not up to much but you don't need to rip out the whole thing. A spiral staircase occupies only a small amount of space but is unsuitable for small children and the elderly. Even some fit adults find spiral staircases unnerving. Carrying a cup of coffee up a spiral is difficult – and forget about moving furniture up or down. If you must install a new stairs to reach an attic conversion or some such thing, use an L-shaped staircase with a break in the steps.

Staircase safety is important. The stairs must be well lit and the carpet very securely fixed. If you're carrying out a renovation and are replastering the walls, it's a good idea to have your electrician put small low-energy LED lights recessed into the wall low down beside each step. These should illuminate the treads, not the risers – you want to see where your foot is falling. There should be a spotlight or overhead light at every landing – or wherever the stairs change direction. Arrange for two-way switches in these locations so that lights can be turned on or off as you go up or down the stairs.

living rooms

COMFORT is more important in a living room than in any other room as we spend so much time there. It's a place to put your feet up but also a room in which to entertain. Many people watch television in the living room. If you *do* watch television, try to keep the set behind closed doors – there are many storage options available.

The key to decorating a living room is to think simple. One good-sized sofa plus as many different occasional chairs as you can accommodate is better than a formal arrangement. Let the room have personality: it's a place for displaying collections or beautiful objects. The point of the living room is to enjoy yourself but comfort shouldn't cancel out style: keep things uncluttered yet interesting.

ask yourself:

- What is the purpose of this room: is it for put-up-your-feet relaxing or formal entertaining? Or perhaps both at different times?

- What kind of atmosphere do you want to create: homey or sophisticated? Something in between is often best.

- Traditional or modern: can the room be a little of both? Maybe use a traditional piece in a modern setting, or vice versa?

- Will the television be the focus of the room? Do you want it to be? If not, how can you hide it?

- How much seating do you need on an everyday basis? How much extra seating will you need if guests come around? From which position will those sitting on the sofa have the best view?

In the family room of this house in Dublin, designed by Milo Fitzgerald, straightforward curtains in a low-key pattern, with goblet pleats to soften the fabric, hang straight and offer a no-fuss solution to dressing the windows.

- Do you also need the room to work as a home office? Does it need to be child-friendly? Is there a corner for reading?

- Have you got enough lighting: lots of lamps or an overhead fitting?

sofa so good

A sofa is one of the largest and potentially most expensive items you'll buy for your home. If you are starting to decorate a living room from scratch, buy a sofa first as it will determine the scale of all your other furnishings.

Regardless of the price range – whether you're buying a sofa from a shop floor or having one specially made – always have the dimensions of your room to hand. Avoid buying a very cheap sofa: it will almost certainly look shabby fast. But neither do you need to spend a fortune: the middle market is very well served when it comes to sofas.

The important elements of sofa (and armchair) design are the depth of the seat, the height between the ground and the top of the seat cushion, and the rake – the slant of the sofa's back. The rake is very important. If you sit on a sofa and slide right out of it, that's because the rake isn't steep enough. Generally a deeper seat is more comfortable. You want to be able to snuggle up on your sofa, not feel you're perched on a ledge. Check the small details: are the seams straight and is it generally well finished?

The easiest way to test the quality of a sofa is to see if the fabric creases when you sit or if the sofa fails to bounce back to its original shape when you stand up. Top-quality sofas offer the most resistance because, whether filled with feathers or foam, they are the most tightly packed. Also look for stability. Sofas should be fairly heavy and solid. Make sure you can remove the sofa covers for cleaning.

window-dressing

When it comes to windows, simple is almost always best. The fabric, the rod and the architecture of the room are the components of curtain choices.

A throw (or woollen blanket) adds contrasting colour and extra texture to a sofa. When folded across the arm, it's ready for use as an aid to getting cosy. Or use a large one spread across the seat and back of the sofa for an instant change of look. A patterned throw brings instant personality to a plain sofa. A similar effect could be achieved by buying a yard-and-a-half of fabric and laying it over the sofa in the same way. Fabric shops often sell off odd pieces of expensive fabrics at bargain prices and these are perfect for this sort of thing. Adding new cushions is the easiest way to make your sofa seem like new.

Left: Armchairs make a corner for reading attractive: try to pair an armchair with a small side-table. Armchairs that are a little wider than normal provide a lot more comfort. White may be more difficult to keep but looks fantastic. Make sure covers can be removed and cleaned easily.

Below left: Legs tend to date a sofa. Look for one with recessed legs. One continuous seat is less fussy and makes a sofa look larger. Multiple back cushions make for great comfort.

Below right: A chaise doesn't take up that much more space than an armchair but brings extra luxury to a room and varies your seating configuration. It juxtaposes nicely with a regular sofa and in combination with a chaise and sofa most rooms would require only an extra chair or two.

If you've any kind of half-way attractive windows, or an interesting view, cover them in as discreet a way as possible. Blinds can be used for privacy. Wooden blinds, especially with contrasting tape, always look smart. Roman blinds in natural linen are a fail-safe solution. Curtains can work well over a Roman blind as this creates a layered, warm look that also helps to regulate the light.

Curtains do add warmth, literally and atmospherically, and are essential in a bedroom for a sense of cocooning. But no matter where they are used in your home, keep curtains straight and unpretentious. Swags and bows usually look ridiculous. Instead, go for a tailored look. If in doubt go for men's suiting colours: camel, navy, grey, white. Let the curtains fade away and bring colour into the room in other ways.

If possible do not buy readymade curtains. There are some exceptions but they rarely look good. Black-out blinds are better than black-out lining, which can deform the shape of the curtains and darken light fabrics.

Curtains should almost always be interlined – pure, raw cotton between the fabric and the ordinary lining. It will make curtains fuller and help them drape better. It's better to go for a cheaper fabric and have it interlined than a more expensive one with ordinary lining.

Find a curtain-maker who offers a complete service: measuring, supply of fabric, making and fitting. Home visits are a must: a good curtain-maker will insist on taking his or her own measurements of your window.

Curtains right across the whole window wall, not just the window opening, make for a dramatic look. The curtain track should sit out from the window and be recessed into the wall on either side. The result is curtaining that dresses the whole wall. Light fabrics, such as muslin and silk viscose, work best because of translucence. Anything else would be too heavy and could make the space feel enclosed.

For a fast change, think about using your existing furniture in a different way. Take one piece out and see what space is created. Rearrange what you have: put the sofa in a different position or put a side-table between two armchairs, anything that shakes things up.

It's usually better to have a large sofa along with unusual, occasional seating than two medium-sized sofas and a bulky armchair. At the SoHo apartment of Cork-born fashion designer Samantha Treacy, a contemporary sofa is softened by cushions made from printed fabric and mixed with classic 1950s and 1960s chairs. In Ireland, we may not have views to rival the Manhattan skyline, but if you do have a beautiful vista at your disposal, don't impinge on it with heavy curtains: use blinds instead if your windows are good-looking enough and you have an adequate heating system. If not, or if you have an old house with draughty windows, buy thermal blinds which are very effective for keeping out the cold.

Right: In John and Karen Redmond's home, a classic square-armed velvet sofa has clean lines that work well in any décor. Cushions in complementary colours dress it and add comfort. An elongated ottoman in front offers a resting place for a book or drink and doubles as extra seating.

Below: Allowing curtains hang a little longer than just touching the floor is always nice (short curtains can look mean) and allows for the shrinkage that will inevitably happen when they're dry-cleaned. Incidentally, note how this room uses a variety of armchairs rather than a sofa. Not for everyone but it works here.

Opposite: Ornate frames add richness and unexpected contrast in a contemporary setting.

Overleaf: Hairdresser John Barrett's West Village apartment in New York has a drop-sided sofa that's well-cushioned and high-backed. A sofa this simple and elegant needs strong accents: note the animal-skin rug (always chic) and weighty stone coffee table.

picture-perfect

How you hang pictures makes a big difference to the overall decoration of a room. Plan your arrangement before you start banging holes in the wall and make sure you have strong-enough hooks and wire.

Stand your pictures around the room and shuffle them about to come up with different combinations. Consider how paintings look against one another, how they appear in relation to fabric colours and furniture and how they fit into the wall space available.

If hanging a group of pictures, lay them out on the floor and move them around to find a good balance. If they differ greatly in size, use the largest as a starting point. A large painting will have a great influence on how the room is going to look and there are probably only a few places it can hang.

Align frames along an invisible grid. Use an imaginary line on the wall – a horizontal line with pictures arranged above or below; or a few vertical lines to make centre-points for column arrangements. There's no science, just what looks balanced. Keep distances between frames the same. Never have pictures too close to one another. Pinpoint the centre of a wall and position your main painting there; it should be at eye level. Work other pictures around it.

Sometimes an uneven pattern can be more interesting than a precise grid or line-up: another approach to picture-ohanging is one that is driven by interest in the pictures themselves rather than simply achieving a decorative effect. This creates a look that reflects the natural growth of a collection and isn't too contrived. Try to keep large images high and more detailed ones lower, so they can be seen more easily. That often works best on a staircase.

The colour of your walls will affect how a picture looks. Traditional oils and works without mounts stand out against dark colours. Paler walls are

better for watercolours and modern works. Patterned wallpaper need strong images in gutsy frames.

Photographs are often best presented uniformly and simply in plain black frames. For a classic look, convert colour photographs to black and white.

showing off collections

Displaying objects you have gathered over the years – boxes, decorative plates, vases, silver – on surfaces such as mantelpieces, side tables and coffee tables makes a home personal. Three or more objects placed together create a more powerful statement than just one or two.

fireplaces and mantelpieces

The fireplace is the focus of most living rooms and symbol of hearth and home. There can be few things more comforting than the flickering flames and sweet-smelling, smouldering wood of an open fire or stove. Fireplaces provide a natural focal point and add architectural interest to a room. It's usually wise to keep an original fireplace because it will probably suit the proportions of the room better than a modern alternative.

If, however, you decide the fireplace has to go, there are many choices open to you. It is comparatively easy to remove one and install another or, for a contemporary look, neaten up the aperture with a plain metal surround. This means there is no fireplace surround or mantelpiece, just a simple opening in the wall. It's become popular to raise such openings almost to eye level so the fire is up off the floor. It's just a question of taste.

Shop around before you buy. Fireplaces can cost thousands and thousands of euro but of course there are many to be had reasonably. Most companies who specialise in selling them will supply the stone, brick or tile surrounds and grate inserts as well. Go to showrooms where you'll have the opportunity to see many designs.

Above left: Group smaller pictures near larger ones for contrast. Unframed artworks have a lovely casual quality.

Above right: A symmetrical hanging pattern is often the most pleasing way of arranging pictures. This fireplace was painted a darker colour than others in the room to bring focus to the monochrome artworks by Alice Maher.

Right: These frames were too white against the wall so a border in dark putty was painted to define them.

Opposite: Display is all about combining objects that sit easily together in terms of scale and style. Here, a mirror and shell at the home of Laragh Stuart.

Big, simple shapes look best on the mantelpiece, but alternate large items with a few smaller ones that draw you in for a closer look. Here, a white vase mirrors the white picture above and stands out against the putty walls. It's always nice to include something natural such as a piece of coral or fresh flowers.

Perhaps the most important thing is that the fireplace be in proportion to your room. Also, it might sound obvious but remember the living room needs to be warm: generally speaking, people are sitting around relaxing, not bustling around creating their own heat. So no matter how efficient your heating system, you will want your fireplace to throw out as much heat as possible. Give the salesperson the dimensions of your room, or better still, have them visit your home.

Work with a professional. Don't attempt to install a fireplace yourself. Consult a professional because you want to make sure the fireplace is installed correctly so it is not a fire hazard.

The mantelpiece can be used to display objects or collections, but edit them carefully – you don't want to weigh down the mantelpiece visually. Just two or three things can be enough. Too many little items together can look like clutter – photographs, flower, figurines and candlesticks. Keep it simple: a parade of white pottery, for example, is always a pleasant grouping.

Avoid a black hole in the grate when the fire is not in use; a stack of firewood is better than looking at a dirty grate. White birch logs are always lovely, if you can get your hands on them, or use an interesting object in summer months.

combining two apartments into one (overleaf)

When a Dublin home-owner bought his neighbour's apartment, he knew it was an opportunity to create a spectacular living space by combining the two apartments so he called on Maria MacVeigh to redesign the space.

There were few limitations structurally, apart from the existing services in fixed positions and the lift shaft that goes through one side of the space. First the two apartments were gutted. With views of the Grand Canal on one side and Percy Place on the other, it was decided that the living areas should be given views over the water, while the two bedrooms should look towards the street.

A collection of photographs and pictures hanging together above a sofa makes for an interesting corner in this living room. The wall, in a darker shade, makes the white borders within the frames stand out.

In redesigning this space, a major concern was to draw sunlight to the darker canal side of the apartment. The answer was to create two wide tunnels that would run from the bright side to the canal side, cutting through a new central 'block' containing the bathrooms, a utility room and storage. The key was to make them wide enough for them not to be considered corridors but a passage from one area to another. Each passage, leading to one of the two bedrooms, successfully brightens the living areas, pictured here. Both are lined in French oak joinery and the floor is also oak. This joinery that wraps around to the main rooms creates a sense of continuity. Doors in the passages open to the bathrooms and storage.

You enter the apartment through a small vestibule which, for privacy, is screened from the living areas by a floor-to-ceiling panel of dark glass. The central fireplace core of the two original apartments divides the living areas. One half is used for watching television and working. The television is recessed into the chimney breast and can be hidden away behind folding panels. On the other side of the fireplace is a seating and dining area with kitchen leading from it. A pelmet disguises the blind mechanism and links the two sides of the room, while a wide bench hanging from the back wall next to the kitchen is the same width as the kitchen countertop. It hides the radiators and provides a resting place for art. From any angle, the eye is drawn to other inviting spaces in the apartment. The colour palette was inspired by the ingredients of the classic Double Decker chocolate bar. Carmel, nougat and dark chocolate are echoed in oak panelling, white walls and dark glass with a bronze tinge.

An Irish-born designer living in London, Ryan McElhinney has, over time, decorated his apartment with a cool mix of vintage and contemporary furniture. He loves the juxtaposition of old and new, so the space is filled with market finds, intriguing artwork and furniture he has made: the brown sofa is second-hand, for example, and the deckchair was found at a market. The lamps he designed are made from salvaged lamp bases sprayed with high-gloss paint. Another sofa is covered in the same grey fabric as the curtains. The floor is resin. This wonderful hard-wearing material is poured and therefore seamless. Nor is it particularly expensive. The soft palette of brown, grey and black works here because of the high ceilings and large windows which make the place bright. Perhaps these colours would not work so well in a darker space. It's very much a man's apartment and what's wonderful about it is that beautiful (but humble) old furniture with history can be appreciated against a clear, elegant backdrop.

dining rooms

A DINING ROOM set aside solely for dining is a space-gobbling luxury most families can't afford. These days, the dining room may be part of the kitchen, a section at the end of the living room, or if it is a separate room, it may double as a study or office. Eating should be relaxing and enjoyable, whether the dining area is a corner of the kitchen or a full-blown formal affair. So don't simply stick a table and chairs in a room; make your dining area as interesting as the rest of your home. A sure sign that you have got it right is when family and friends linger at the table long after the meal is over, rather than look around hopefully in search of a more comfortable place to relax.

If you do not have the luxury of a dining room used just for dining – and most of us do not – the trick is to make your dining table look as if it's not a dining table most of the time. This means not having a table surrounded by chairs – except, of course, when you are actually going to use it for eating. The problem of where to put those extra chairs is not really so very difficult to resolve. You could buy chairs that act as occasional chairs; they can be distributed throughout bedrooms and the hall if it is big enough, then brought together when needed. These days you do not have to go for matching suites of dining furniture, any more than you have to choose three-piece suites for the living room. No one will look askance if you have a makeshift table disguised by a floor-length tablecloth, painted or lacquered ex-kitchen chairs and a Victorian wardrobe for glass and china storage. Why should they? What you are achieving with such a happy mix is very much more personal and, therefore, more interesting than the blandness of the careful match.

ask yourself:

*   What is the maximum number of people you would want to seat regularly?

Colour plays its part in this room: soft green is a perfect dining colour. The walls of this Dublin apartment are covered with textured paper. Wallpaper with a grain or shot with fabric smoothes out imperfect walls and gives a richness paint cannot. Accent lighting in this dining room, in the form of white wall-lights and lamps, gently creates mood and drama. More decorative than utilitarian, lighting such as this should be kept at a low level. These lights are themselves beautiful accessories and can be installed on a dimmer switch so they can be adjusted. Note the comfy chairs: they're almost armchairs and wonderful for protracted meals. Flowers lend a decorative note to a dinner table and dictate the mood of a gathering. But don't stress about flowers – life is too short for contrived arrangements.

The efficient use of space involves having your home function in the ways that will best suit your family. Most people these days find that the traditional roles of rooms are no longer relevant. This is true of the kitchen, in particular, which has partially taken over the role both of living room and dining room. You therefore need to make sure the kitchen is organised and furnished to cope with its wider role. The dining room, on the other hand, can be used for different functions at different times. For example, it could also be a home office if work-related items and a computer can be easily hidden away in a large unit with folding doors; or it could become a games room, again if there is adequate storage for things to be tidied away quickly. It may be possible to make a room dual-purpose simply by choosing furniture carefully: a table that is extendable, stackable chairs or, if you have space, perhaps a neat sofa-bed can be included so the dining room can double as an impromptu guest bedroom. The approach you take will obviously depend on the size of the room and the purposes to which it will be put.

• Would a rectangular table or a round one fit the space best?

• Will you be hosting a lot of formal dinners or more casual gatherings?

• Do you have multiple light sources?

• Where will lamps rest?

• How can you soften hard-wearing flooring?

The dining room, whether it's part of a kitchen or a separate space, is the place where families gather to share food, company and laughter. It needs to be adaptable: a place to celebrate or make a simple meal a special event. Success lies in comfort. Nobody wants to sit on a chair that's too hard or that doesn't support your back in the right way. A dining area needs little more than a good-sized table, chairs and storage. Buy a quality table, preferably extendable, large enough to accommodate any eventuality, or as large as your room can take. Think about chairs that don't match the table for a more interesting look. Find a storage piece for everyday convenience.

Don't feel obliged by necessity or convention to furnish all in one style. Mix, say, 18th-century pieces with the very modern; country pieces with glass and chrome; contemporary with early Victorian; a nice Regency side-table with a leather chair. If you can't afford a good antique table, get a second-hand junk table and do what you can with it: paint it, strip it, or cover it with cloth. Then invest as much as you can in comfortable chairs. You can still achieve a traditional feeling without having to spend a lot of money on antique chairs. Not particularly nice reproduction chairs can be lacquered in unexpected colours. And so on. Antique furniture gets a great facelift just by being set against a clean backdrop.

If space is short, a round table takes up a smaller area than a square or rectangular one. Folding chairs can help too but make sure there is really

Left: Conventional wisdom may be that small rooms need small pieces of furniture but the owners of this house did just the opposite in their dining room, hanging an oversized old light fitting over the table. Found at an auction and lit with low-watt bulbs, it brings drama into an otherwise quiet room. The chairs around the table are all different, sourced in various places. They're upholstered in different fabrics but are all about the same height to reduce visual chaos.

Right: Style doesn't need to cost a lot: using chairs that are not really dining chairs can be fun. These are old garden chairs that the young owner had spruced up. This is quite a simply decorated room but it's full of interesting things, personal to the owner. The lace stretched across the window is quirky but gives privacy too. The colour scheme is kept to a lovely palette of green, white and back. Open shelving is more than a place to stow your goods: with a little creative arranging, it's a place to show them off. Here, shelves are used to hold important everyday things such as tableware, table linen, glassware, and cutlery. Display makes art of the everyday objects that please you the most.

enough room for the table when all the chairs are in position. Check that the chairs are comfortable. On some fold-away designs the back can seem too far forward so that it's impossible to sit at ease with the right amount of back support. Others are not very stable if occupied by someone of generous proportions. Your style can be more individual if you have a separate dining room. It will depend on the proportions of the room and of other furniture if your dining area is part of another room.

Lighting should be soft but bright enough for people to see what they're eating. The light must never be so bright that it kills atmosphere. The old classic is a rise-and-fall pendant light that gives just the right level of illumination and can be run from a dimmer switch when you want a soft background light to complement the glow of candles. The sideboard, dresser or serving area could be lit by wall lights. There are, of course, all sorts of chandeliers available in brass, iron, wood, wrought-iron and crystal. The sideboard or serving table needs to be well lit but even if you use table lamps, use spots placed in the ceiling and on a dimmer. There are many subtle types of spotlights available now, not just brass rings. These can highlight pictures or a fireplace. Take any collections you have into consideration when planning lighting: a lit display is always very dramatic.

In a dining room, candlelight is the definitive accent light. Use a mix of pillars, tapers and tea-lights on the table and beyond to fill the room with a warm glow. Don't go over the top, though: you're guests don't want to feel as if they're dining in a church. A fire is always a great success in a dining room: the combination of firelight and candlelight puts people in a mellow mood. Plenty of mirrors on the walls will refract the flickering light.

There is any number of suitable treatments for walls in a dining room as there is not going to be much wear and tear. A clean neutral paint colour means the room will be adaptable. Simplicity is the essence of style: a neutral colour palette on walls means that your room can shift gears effortlessly and you will be able to reinvent the space with seasonal decorations, loose covers for chairs or changes of linen. If you like the simplicity of white

The artwork was the starting point for this room – colours picked out in classic Eames Eiffel Tower chairs that sit around a Knoll table. The small table is extendable.

Above left: Carpet, wood, stone and tiles are not the only flooring choices. The owners of this house in Clontarf laid a polished concrete floor in their dining area. It is mixed with coloured stones for interest and has under-floor heating to take the cold edge off the material.

Above right: Colour could be introduced with wall-coverings

Right: A high black-gloss table makes for a glamorous look but is not for homes with children: sticky fingers will mean constant cleaning.

Left: If you have a big space and want to separate the dining area visually from the living space, a partial room-divider could be the answer. This house has timber-framed glass panels that don't block natural light but make the dining area just a little bit more intimate. It's a grown-up room with sophisticated touches, including a large wide-framed mirror that, because it's painted the same shade of white as the walls, is almost like an architectural feature.

There are houses for different seasons. This is the dining area in a home of a couple with teenage children. It opens off the kitchen and is a practical room with aged porcelain tiles and sturdy leather seating. A 1960s light fitting adds some character. The advantages of a circular table go without saying: it is conducive to conversation and, if you've got the space, a nice contrast to the straight lines of a room.

but still want *some* colour, consider beige or grey. Beige gets a bad press for being boring but it's the perfect colour to show off your artwork and furniture. A dining room is about people around a table: they should be the focus, not over-elaborate decoration. Textured wallpapers can also work well in a dining room, adding to a rich warm atmosphere. What pleases the hand usually pleases the eyes as well. The selection available now is wide-ranging and effects include leather, bamboo, woven and gold leaf. Wallpapers such as these are a great way to introduce depth to the room.

I personally don't think it's a good idea to have carpet in the dining area where it picks up smells and gets dirtier more quickly than in most places, since people do, without fail, drop food and drink. But I have nothing against rugs of any description. A wooden or tiled floor is probably better: soften it with a rug which can always be cleaned. A hard floor does mean a certain amount of clattering noise from chairs being pulled up to the table and pushed back again. This can be minimised by padding the bottom of the chair-legs.

When it comes to window treatments, remember that very heavy fabric is inclined to pick up food smells and harbour them. Instead, keep curtaining light. Perhaps curtains aren't necessary at all.

Once you have decided which facts you have to face and whittled down the possibilities in relation to to space, family and pocket, you can decide much more easily on the feeling you would like to introduce. Clearly, in a family dining room that's part of a kitchen or living room and with several small children to cater for, you are not likely to go for any sort of exotic or delicate items. Tough materials and furniture are a better choice – at least for a couple of years, But this can create a feeling of its own. Even if you don't have small children, there may be other limitations that turn out to be more limiting than inspiring. Here's where it pays to borrow a little inspiration. Think about which restaurants have made you feel comfortable and at ease – maybe there are some elements you could recreate?

Interior designer Deirdre Danaher, who owns this house, often entertains at home and chose comfortable Danish 'Moller' chairs with woven seats. The Moller is a great chair because the shape is so open, yet it feels like an armchair. In small spaces, avoid chairs with tall backs: they don't necessarily make a chair more comfortable and really block off a great deal of a room. The bench on the other side of the table came from a church. The glass table is narrower than a normal table. It's very long and suits the shape of the room. A lot of people choose a table that's too small because they're afraid to clutter a room, but don't forget that everything happens at the table. Avoiding using suites of furniture in small spaces: have interesting pieces that don't match but have some relation to one another. The dining table here, for example, has iron legs that complement the long bench next to it. The two large prints are by artist Brian Kennedy. Using big art in a small space adds a bit of punch to a room. Also, because this dining area is part of the kitchen, using art makes it feel less kitcheny.

a smart grey dining-room

This dining room (*opposite*) is a very successful mix: the furniture is modern but the general effect and feel are formal enough for the scale of the period room. The table, chairs and sideboard are all wood with a glossy black finish. The grey walls are relieved by the original white marble fireplace and the pale wood floor. Decorating with grey might seem oppressive, but the trick is to balance it with white. The white seat-cushions and artworks also provide a nice accent. Grey is a great neutral and there are many shades from which to choose, many a good deal paler than the one here. Grey makes people stand out and, in a dining room, food. Green is a also good colour to combine with grey.

Light is all-important in this room: a subdued background light comes from the classic 1930s table lamp. People should look good at night and soft, diffused light is essential in a dining room. The sideboard on which the lamp rests is perfect for china and cutlery. If you are buying a sideboard, choose a neat low one that doesn't intrude on the room. It doesn't have to be a star piece of furniture.

Speaking of china, glasses, cutlery and linen, these items are as much a part of dining-room decoration as the furniture and wall colour. There's no point getting all the other decorative details perfect if your plates and knives and forks are all wrong. It doesn't matter whether they are family heirlooms or bargains from a market stall; if they're right for the setting that's all that counts.

When you're choosing china, think as much about shapes and sizes as about colour and pattern. Do they come in a wide range to suit all your needs? Are they going to be your everyday set or used only on special occasions? Will they stand up to family wear and tear but look too sturdy for dinner parties? Are they all dishwasher/oven/freezer-proof? Do you want to be able to add to them over the years or is the manufacturer likely to discontinue that particular pattern? Good table linen is also essential to show off the food and to add to the atmosphere. By changing tablecloths and napkins you can alter the feeling and style of the room quite spectacularly without going to a lot of expense.

Right: Neutral walls and furnishings in a dining space make a room feel spacious and allow you to add accessories of any colour. This classic Saarinen dining table and chairs are as cool today as they were when they were designed in the 1960s. Wood floors and colourful artwork give warmth to what might otherwise be an austere space.

Opposite: A kitchen-dining room that combines the new with the weathered and the antique is timeless. Defy the expected by setting old furniture against the sleek finishes of a modern table: opposites always attract. These old chairs have been painted a fun turquoise colour. The red lampshade is a nice link to the red canvas. This room is a hang-out space, with the kitchen at one end. The floor has been covered with inexpensive plywood panels, painted the same off-white shade as the walls so it looks molded and creates a streamlined finish.

Below: The other side of the same room.

kitchens

WE LIVE more casually than ever before and the kitchen has become the most multi-functional space in a home. Now it often opens directly into other rooms and is not closed off from the rest of the house so it has to work decoratively with these other spaces.

An effective kitchen is one that makes the most of the space available. It should be functional but aesthetically pleasing, modern and not a snapshot of the past. Kitchens are rarely inexpensive but that doesn't stop savvy people from making the best of what their budget will allow. An alternative way to get a kitchen that doesn't cost the earth is to buy flat-pack and install yourself. Of course, this takes time and hard graft on your part but by opting for this rather than pre-built and installed units – although the quality may not be the best – you could save yourself a lot of money.

Whatever kitchen you opt for it's important to make sure you choose matching or complementary accessories to highlight the colouration in the room. Good kitchen design is, in essence, about common sense. Think about what you use your kitchen for and how busy it can get. The aim is to make sure that the food preparation area, the cooking area and the kitchen sink are not be too far apart. A good kitchen design will place the fridge between the main entrance and the main cooking area for easy access. Try to avoid locating the fridge or freezer next to the kitchen hob or oven as this will reduce its efficiency.

In terms of how your kitchen looks, the marketplace is overflowing with products that answer every style idea and price point. With all the options available, the best approach is to keep it simple. A good recipe is clean, pale Shaker-style cabinets, a splashback of white rectangular tiles, pale marble countertops and stainless-steel appliances for contrast. Choose

small nickel knobs or handles that are unobtrusive. You don't need a lot of colour or fancy decorative elements: life going on within the kitchen will being colour.

Neither is it a good idea to decorate a kitchen around a theme. You don't live in Provence, so don't do a Provencal kitchen. Stick to simple and classic. You know it won't date any time soon and you'll be living with the choice you made for many years – it's not like a sofa or curtains that can be replaced easily. What's new in decorating is best kept out of this room but that doesn't mean it has to be dull or boring.

Creating a new kitchen from scratch is an expensive luxury but you can update a kitchen by changing a couple of things: have cabinets painted with a clean semi-gloss white (get a professional to do this); change the knobs or handles; buy new appliances if you can; retile the splashback and paint the walls. Refresh a tired sink with new taps. Paint the inside of glass-fronted cabinets. Put up a simple display shelf for your cookbooks or collectable dishware. Replace old curtains with wooden blinds. Revive a wood floor with super-durable enamel outdoor paint. Install under-cabinet lighting – easy to do with all-inclusive packs. Change the bulb in the overhead fitting to give softer, warmer light or put a dimmer switch on it.

ask yourself:

- What is the main purpose of your kitchen? Is it just for cooking or is it for family gatherings as well? Do you have a large-enough table or need one that expands?

- What are your goals – update or renovate? Are they realistic in terms of time and budget?

- Are you a serious cook? Do you need any double appliances? Or an extra-large freezer?

This Churchtown (Dublin) kitchen has no high cabinets, just open shelving that make the room seem more spacious. The high table is more than the usual breakfast bar; it is a proper eating space. The table merges into an island with storage drawers. Drawers are almost always better than presses as it's easy to access everything and there is no bending to root at the back of a cupboard. Note the small neat knobs and plain simple doors with a little recessed detail. A low splashback rises from the countertop. Pendant lights are always good over an island. Neutrals are practical and 'safe', which is important if you plan to resell. Creamy cabinetry, surfaces and appliances mean that everything coordinates easily.
Light colours and smooth, reflective surfaces maximise light and enhance the sense of space.

Chef Monique
McQuaid's kitchen
in Greystones has a
back wall papered
with distinctive
wallpaper. A
toughened glass
panel over the
wallpaper rises the
to the same height
as a conventional
splashback to
protect it from
cooking splashes.
Wallpaper can
work in a kitchen
if used with care.
The worktop is
also toughened
glass. The white
units were bought
inexpensively
from Ikea and put
together in an
afternoon. Shop
around and you can
find great value:
for instance, the
sink in this kitchen
is from B&Q. The
walls of the kitchen
extension are angled
to connect with the
original house and
this makes for a
room that feels out
of the ordinary. The
floorboards, too,
were deliberately
placed out of
line with the
central island.

Above: This small kitchen has two sides: the sink area has a black glass splashback, matt granite work surface and storage beneath; on the other side, a unit houses a stainless-steel oven and microwave. Stainless-steel appliances will update any kitchen. Parquet flooring such as in this room is expensive but worth it.

Right: This kitchen in Blackrock is nicely broken up: that is, it isn't laid out in a uniform way. The countertop is American walnut (surprisingly easy to maintain) and, in a nice contrast, the skirting is stainless steel to match a pull-down door to the left of the stove. Stainless-steel or brushed-steel finishes are durable, hygienic and stylish. They coordinate well with appliances and reflect light. The wood floor has been stained with a dark high-gloss finish. Hardwood floors really stand up to the comfort test. Save money by retaining existing flooring and resurfacing or resealing. Cork, hardwood or bamboo floors offer warmth, cushioning, durability and style, but require resanding and resealing every so often to withstand traffic, splashes and spills.

- Do you prefer open or closed storage? Or a mix of the two? Are you neat enough for glass-panelled cabinet doors?

- Do you have enough counter space?

- Do you entertain a lot? Need extra storage for glasses and plates?

- Do you need a desk to deal with paperwork and bills?

- Do you have sufficient light over the countertops?

layout

Most kitchen companies will advise on layout so to save you time and stress consider a kitchen design-and-installation package. But if you decide to do most of the work yourself, there are a few things to keep in mind. Be guided by common sense and convenience. Work out what's annoying about your existing kitchen – lack of light, bench space or power outlets, a single sink, a difficult-to-clean stovetop. Attempt to iron out those problems in the new design.

Don't be overly constrained by the existing configuration. Sometimes pipes, gas-lines, electrics, walls and windows can be repositioned with less effort and expense than you'd expect. But changing service points for major appliances can cost a great deal of money so if you don't have an unlimited budget, your design choices may be somewhat restricted. Save money by retaining some fittings (resurfacing or refitting as needed). If clever design can't solve space problems, consider expanding the kitchen via a buffet-style breakfast bar or island bench.

Plan your kitchen taking the natural pattern of people's movement into consideration. Allow a comfortable distance between each of the kitchen's functions: storage, cooking, workspace, waste-handling and washing up. Position the sink, fridge and oven so that they form a 'work triangle'. Note that left or right-handedness affects layout: for a good right-handed flow, position in this order (right to left): dishwasher and sink, workspace,

Stone and tile are waterproof, durable and easy to clean. However, some stone floors can stain, so have them properly sealed. For a practical, cost-effective alternative, consider new-generation linoleum: it's hardwearing, flexible and available in a myriad styles. Consider the slip rating of your kitchen flooring as accidents do happen.

cooking unit, utility storage. Position the sink, drainage and dishwasher first. They will comprise the biggest single unit in your kitchen. Sinks are usually placed against an outside wall under a window for convenient drainage and good natural lighting. The dishwasher should be close to the crockery and cutlery. It should also be away from doorways and the stove, so it can be loaded easily. Locate the food preparation areas between the oven and the sink. If you're gutting your kitchen, consider installing extra power-points at the time, as it is very expensive to get new ones put in when all the other work has been completed.

windows

To increase natural light, consider resizing existing windows, adding skylights or opening the space to living, dining or outdoor areas. There is no point at all in elaborate window coverings in the kitchen. They become dirty, greasy and get in the way. It is far better to use blinds, if you really need something. Fabric should be easily washed or cleaned: cotton, or vinylised cotton for roller blinds. Otherwise use Venetian blinds in wood which can be easily wiped, or wooden shutters, or no covering at all.

lighting

The same rules for planning light fittings apply in the kitchen as every-where else in the home: general light to see by; work-light to work by; and an accent light to show off anything particularly worth looking at. The special rule of a kitchen is to make sure that there is light over every work surface so that you never have to work in your own shadow. Insert a general pendant light or spotlights for the overall light; fix light below upper cabinets to shine directly on to the worktop and try to install special lights over the stove and sink. Make sure the overall lights are on a dimmer switch: when you eat in the kitchen, you'll want to be able to turn down the glare. Independent switches for each light will make it easier to create the right atmosphere. Remember to position switches and outlets with practicality in mind: light-switches next to doors; multiple outlets above countertops designated for appliances.

Always have a vase of fresh flowers on display somewhere in the eating area. Even greenery cut from the garden can create an impact.

Candles transform the atmosphere, especially if you eat at the kitchen table. They place the focus firmly on the table and the conversation. Keep a supply of tea-lights, fat church candles and large pillars and a variety of candle holders in your cupboard.

Put up a wall panel of either cork or plywood painted with blackboard paint for shopping lists and reminders and for displaying children's artwork and party invitations.

A combined radio and CD player is a good companion for kitchen-users of all ages. Music is an important backdrop that can greatly enhance the atmosphere.

A galley kitchen with simple white units and granite countertop is partly separated from the main living area of this apartment but has an open cut-out section that connects to a breakfast bar and the living space beyond. This keeps goings-on in the kitchen fairly hidden but still connected to the main room – an alternative to having the space totally open. White units, black countertops and stainless-steel appliances are dateless and inexpensive to achieve, albeit not the most revolutionary look.

This kitchen was designed by architect Sterrin O'Shea for a house in Rathgar in Dublin. We eat, entertain, do homework and even cook in the kitchen. The room has come a long way from its utilitarian past but it's still best to keep things functional rather than overly decorative. This kitchen is an elegant blank canvas for family life. Why live in the past with a pseudo-traditional kitchen? This is busiest room in the house, so keep the design clean and cleanable.

worktops and sinks

If space permits, choose a double-bowl sink, with deep bowls for pot-washing. For right-handers, the most natural placement of the washing area is to the left of the workspace, with a dish-drainer and dishwasher to the left of the sink. Consider adding an in-sink garbage disposal unit (unless you prefer to compost your organic waste) and an inbuilt water filter.

Worktops have to be as durable as floors, able to withstand chopping, hot utensils and spills and still be good to look at. Formica or plastic laminate is not a good idea: you must be careful not to chop directly onto it or to put down hot saucepans. Once damaged it is extremely difficult to put right. Ceramic tiles, which can be continued up the space between countertop and unit, come in a huge range of colours and styles and can look very fresh. However, the grouting can easily get discoloured so it might be better to start with dark grouting from the beginning. You also need to be wary of putting down very hot pots and pans; this might cause the ceramic to crack. Wood countertops are sturdy and look good but they are not very practical near the sink because they can warp and the grain can rise up. If you are using wood as a continuous work surface, introduce some variety; incorporate some marble or stone or surround the sink with stainless steel. Corian is a mineral-filled plastic that looks a little like marble but is very practical. It's available in many colours.

Generally, though, although natural stone countertops can be expensive, they're worth the investment in terms of beauty and durability. Carrera marble is the material of the moment for countertops and splashbacks. This classic marble with a grey vein is bright and fresh, throwing light into a kitchen rather than soaking it up, as dark granites do. It looks good against units in any shade of grey or blue-green and can look stunning used as a ceiling-high splashback. Carrera technically shouldn't be used as a countertop as it's prone to staining, but it can be protected and sealed. Some staining will occur but you've got to think of this as adding character and not be too precious about it.

Existing kitchen units can be given a facelift without the expense of replacing them entirely. New doors can be put on the old carcases, or old doors can be removed, sanded down and then painted and varnished. If the surfaces are laminate you will need to use a specialist paint or primer. Talk to a good joiner about possibilities.

As kitchens become more multi-functional, the conventional concept of fitted units arranged in a traditional layout is increasingly open to revision. Influential kitchen designers have produced bespoke kitchens that barely look like cooking areas. Relaxed, graciously proportioned spaces furnished with flowing curves, delicate woodwork and sympathetic colour disguise function if that's your wish (and you have the money to spend).

Provide ample work surfaces in key areas: next to the fridge and oven and on both sides of the hob and sink. For safety and efficiency, allow adequate space for preparation and serving and at least 450mm set-down next to the fridge and wall oven. A good working countertop height is 80-95cm high. Avoid positioning a workspace or cooking unit in a corner.

Kitchen units in a traditional style look fresh when used with a modern element. For example, tongue-and-groove units painted in a contemporary colour, such as slate-grey, look modern. If painted bland cream, they might look too predictable. A kitchen with this kind of unit can be livened up with an interesting countertop, such as unusual wood (sweet gum tree is the new thing). Marble and wood can be mixed together to good effect: the unit countertops in marble perhaps; the island in wood. Stainless steel remains an easy and practical way to modernise a kitchen when used as a splashback or trimming detail.

If your kitchen is open to another room, for instance part of the living or dining space, make units as discreet as possible. Use press-and-release handles and don't have any fussy details. This will help to make the units 'fade away'.

storage

People are always complaining that they do not have enough workspace or cupboards in their kitchens but it may well be that what they really need is better organised storage. Look at your kitchen countertops. Are you using them to best advantage? Or are they so cluttered up that there isn't any real space to work on? If clutter is your problem, be ruthless and get rid of anything that you haven't used for the last six months, and put everything else away in a cabinet or cupboard somewhere. If there doesn't seem to be any room to keep storage jars, canisters, cooking tools and so on, you might need to add more shelves and hooks. You can often use the space between the bottom of the wall-hung cabinets and the countertop to put up small shelves which will take a variety of objects. If your cabinets seem to be constantly overcrowded, open up all the doors and look at the contents with a critical eye. If there are items that you hardly ever use, remove them to more remote storage areas away from work areas. Seldom-used items such as ham-boiling pots, turkey-roasting pans, fish kettles and picnic baskets might well be parted from day-to-day items. Ditto appliances. You could also consider buying a small-scale butcher's block that will serve as a mini-island or be placed against a wall.

Left: Introduce a natural element to a glossy all-white kitchen with a plain wooden panel. Positioning it vertically gives a modern edge and adds height by drawing the eye upwards. Place it away from the cooking and sink area to avoid warping. This is a small kitchen in a house in Drumcondra in Dublin: depending on your lifestyle, you may not need an awfully large space. A separate hob and oven may be pricier than a single unit but will allow better workflow. Place the oven at a maximum height of 90cm above floor level, out of reach of children and at a good ergonomic height for adults. Microwaves should be no higher than 75mm below your shoulder, so that you are not struggling with heavy, hot containers.

Right: An island provides additional work and storage space in a single line of layout (where units run along one wall). It also gives focus to a kitchen and acts as a place where the family gathers. An island works best in a larger kitchen where its presence does not impede movement between the sink, cooker and fridge. It also provides a possible site for the hob or sink (although both are better on an outside wall). You could also incorporate a small eating bar for snacks and breakfast.

floors

Kitchen floors need to be tough enough to withstand all sorts of spills, grease and damp, comfortable to stand on for long periods and handsome to look at. The choice of floor covering very much depends on the sort of style you have set yourself. Slate is marvellous to look at but at a marvellous price, and there is an enormous choice in ceramic and stone tiles. Generally, something fairly pale is best as it will open up the room. Large sizes also tend to make a floor seem larger. Stone, slate or ceramic treatments can be as hard on the feet as they are on the eye so have under-floor heating rigged up when they are being laid. If both the price and hardness of these floors bother you, rubber floors are soft underfoot, durable and available in almost any colour. Better still, they are affordable. Wood treated with polyurethane to withstand spills and grease can look great, specially in a kitchen that's also a living space – wood somehow makes it seem less kitcheny. Old wood floors can be spruced up with paint and protected with extra coats of varnish. When you are choosing flooring for a kitchen and dining space, make sure the surface is suitable for both functions, or visually separate one are from another by using different types of flooring. For example, if you have stone tiles in the kitchen, they may be rather cold on the feet for dinner guests lingering over coffee, as well as being noisy when chairs scrape across them. You may find that people are encouraged to use the room as more of a gathering place if the floor of the dining area is covered with a colourful rug.

Kitchen seating doesn't always have to mean a conventional table and chairs. An American-style diner booth brings both fun and colour to a corner. A good general upholsterer should be able to make one for you.

Designer Ryan McElhinney's small galley kitchen is from Ikea. The doors are made from fumed oak. The pale resin floor provides a nice contrast to the dark wood. Window treatments in kitchens should be kept simple: a blind of some sort or nothing at all. This kitchen opens into a living area: kitchens like this need to feel less kitcheny than those that are separate rooms. Here this is achieved by the luxury finish (if not great expense) of the units. They look more like furniture than anything else.

bedrooms

Originally four tiny rooms, this bedroom is now one large space with the attic 'reclaimed'. A steel girder is left exposed as a raw feature. The room is separated from the adjoining en-suite by a glass-panelled frame that has the effect of allowing light into both areas and making the whole space seem larger. It's a clever way to create a division when privacy isn't an issue. Furniture in a bedroom can be as eclectic as you wish: note the bedside tables, chest of drawers and lamp which all vary in style and result in a room that's personal and interesting. In general, don't put too much of anything of the same style into a room as you might go off it. Trust your instincts and mix and match.

YOUR BEDROOM should be about comfort and beauty. It's the space you wake up in and the last place you see before the end of the day. In a way, it's the easiest room to decorate. Serenity is key, so paint the walls pale, calm shades. White can be bleak so choose a white with a pink tint or go mad and pick a proper pale pink. It's a very flattering colour, warm yet light. The consensus is that bedrooms should be restful rather than dramatic and be capable of looking both warm and cool, depending on the season.

Choose a really good bed, be it a divan or a mattress that sits in a frame. The way any bedroom is decorated depends on the lifestyle of those who use it. But we all need the same basic ingredients. Your bed is obviously the most important. Restful sleep is impossible on a bed that is lumpy, uncomfortable or too small, so it is worth spending a little money. A good bed will give only so many years of comfort: if you haven't bought a new one in ten years, it's time to update.

The type of bed you buy depends on your individual needs and preferences. You will often see beds described as 'orthopaedic' – but as any orthopaedic surgeon will tell you, there is no such thing. A bed described as orthopaedic simply means that it has a firm mattress. This is not necessarily good for someone suffering from back problems: check with your doctor before buying a new bed. Look for a bed with layers of small nests of memory foam as these respond better to the shape of your body. The comfort factor of a bed depends on the mattress being able to hold the spine in its normal position. If the bed is too hard, the body will slide downwards; if it is too soft, the heavier parts of your body will sink into the mattress. The only way to see if a new bed is comfortable is to try before you buy.

Above left: Neutral colours may seem boring in other rooms, but they work for a bedroom in which you want to rest. You do not need to stimulate the eye with strong colours.

Above right: Lining walls in fabric isn't easy to perfect but when done well, it's sumptuous and comforting. When a low-key, light fabric is used, the look is traditional but not cloying. Curtains in matching material makes sense.

Right: An upholstered headboard is a good-looking classic and an affordable way to achieve a finished appearance with a divan bed. If you are using a very colourful fabric, keep the rest of the room clean and white. Have a cushion cover made in the same fabric to pull the look together.

I favour a divan with a upholstered headboard rather than a mattress in a bed frame as it's less dominating of a room. Position the bed so that it has the best view to make every night feel good. In a small room it's a clever idea to buy a bed that is slightly higher than normal. I'm not sure why it works; it just does. A higher bed gives depth to a small room.

ask yourself:

- Do you need to rip everything out or can you spruce up the room without major changes?

- Do you like to wake up in a bright and sunny space or would something darker be more your thing?

- Which wall colour would be soothing and tranquil for you?

- What about carpet? It's nice to wake up to something warm underfoot.

- Would you like a bed you climb into or one that's low?

- Can you fit a chair, stool or bench so that you can sit and put your shoes on?

- Do you read in bed? Could you have high wall-lights?

- What do you need by your bedside? Maybe you don't need a conventional locker with drawers?

- If you must have a television, is there some way you can hide it when it's not in use?

bedlinen

How you dress your bed adds to its appeal and comfort. You can, of course, change the look of the room by using different throws, duvets and pillows. A down or synthetic-down duvet is the one-step way to dress your bed.

A good mattress should be a priority. If you haven't bought a new one in ten years, it's time to update. Look for those with layers of small 'nests' of memory foam as they respond better to the shape of your body. Go to department stores or showrooms where you can lie on each bed and see how it feels. Everyone's definition of comfortable is different.

Go though your wardrobe at least three times a year and take a refuse sack of clothes to the Simon Community. You don't have to purge completely; just aim to keep the level the same. We all buy so many inexpensive clothes now that when new clothes come in, old stuff should go out.

It adds height and plushness. A throw tossed casually at the end of a bed adds texture, colour and interest. It's also great for those times when you want to curl up and read or watch TV.

A higher thread count doesn't mean better-quality bedlinen. A 400-thread-count from a good brand is much better than a 700-thread-count from another. It's all about the quality of cotton the manufacturer uses. Linens that are made in Europe tend to be of top-quality fibre and are therefore very hardwearing. Before buying, look and see where something is made: Indian and Chinese cottons are not good. Always feel the fabric – it should feel cold, smooth and crisp. I've come across 800-thread-count sheets that feel like cardboard because they're made from short-fibre cotton.

lighting

Bedroom lighting needs to be a combination of general light and directional light for reading, making-up, dressing or writing. Make sure that there is an electrical socket on each side of the bed. Dual controls for general lighting are a good idea as you can switch on as you enter the room, then switch off by the bed when other lamps are lit. Bedside lamps should be tall enough to shine on a book, but not to the other side of the bed where your partner may be trying to sleep. Small lamps which can be angled or dimmed are worth considering if one of you is a dedicated night reader. If there is a chair in the room, a table lamp on a side table, or a floor-light behind the chair provides the right level of illumination for relaxing, reading or sewing. Light for dressing can come from recessed ceiling bulbs. These are at their most useful when fitted with a dimmer as the light level can be increased when you want to see how you look and decreased when all that is needed is a soft overall glow.

storage and furniture

Wardrobes should be functional and in a fade-away colour. Declutter: go though your wardrobe at least three times a year and take a refuse sack of clothes to the Simon Community. You don't have to purge completely: just aim to keep the level the same. We all buy so many inexpensive clothes now that when new clothes come in, old stuff should go out.

Mix family heirlooms with reproduction and Asian furniture. It doesn't matter where something is from as long as you like it. Things that don't come close to matching often work really well together.

Above left: Always run wardrobes right to the ceiling so there is no wasted space. Use the high shelves for suitcases and things that aren't in use every day. Have plenty of drawers and a built-in shoe rack. In this room, the wardrobes take up the full length of one wall and have a pale high-gloss finish to reduce their impact. Ideally, have a light inside that comes on when the doors are opened; even the cheapest supplier should be able to provide this.

Above right: If a room is small, like this one, the easiest way to give an impression of space is to keep everything very neutral. That allows you to use different bedlinen to change the mood. The white walls show off artwork better too.

Left: This is more than a headboard: it's the focus of the room. The padded panels sit behind a smaller headrest with a shelf above for books and trinkets. Tall lamps are best for beside a bed as they shine light down on to whatever you're reading. Ideally it's best to have a chair in a bedroom but if space is an issue, a bench at the end of a bed works almost as well for putting on shoes. Pick up accents from the room in bedlinen and layer up the colour connection with cushions and bedspreads.

If you want to avoid clothes draped over chairs and piles of spare linen and pillows cramping your style, you need to think ahead. As with kitchen planning, it's worth listing what you need to store and working out how much hanging and drawer space is required. Don't forget shoes, bags and luggage, books, magazines, photograph albums and even CDs if you want your bedroom to be a bolthole where you can escape to read or listen to music. If you are starting from scratch, you can opt for fitted furniture or free-standing designs or a combination of the two. If there are already cupboards in place, a new paint finish and updated interior fittings will help improve the look and the usefulness.

Additional items – a bed-end chest or a multi-drawer cabinet, for example – can also provide crucial extra storage. Think laterally – you don't have to restrict yourself to furniture specifically designed for bedrooms. If space is at a premium in your main living areas, the bedroom may be able to accommodate discreet bookshelves or even a small desk area. This approach particularly suits guest bedrooms, which can double up as a study or home office.

Before buying bulky dressers or armoires, make sure you're getting the most out of your wardrobe – especially when it comes to hanging space. You can always add drawer or shelf units but it's harder to change the rods.

Consider what you need to access on a daily basis versus every few months. Your favourite walking shoes should be front and centre, whereas those strappy Manolo Blahniks can be stashed in their boxes on an upper shelf for special occasions. Shoe cubes, tiered tie racks and slide-out laundry bins help keep things tucked away but easily accessible.

Other furniture is best mismatched: beside lockers, a chair, dressing-table, lamps and a tall mirror. Don't overfurnish a bedroom: keep as much free floor-space as possible. Let the décor in your bedroom evolve. Don't make a shopping list: look at what you've got and add to it. That means that when you see something

Right: Warm colours always work in a bedroom. Carpet equals comfort and is the best floor treatment unless you have a particular preference for wood or some other material. Play with scale: here a small ethnic chair surprises you and adds some humour.

Below: This specially-made oak floating bed incorporates a headboard that runs the width of the bedroom. Note too that the blind is recessed and neatly hidden away behind a plaster pelmet.

beautiful, you have an excuse to buy it. Mix family heirlooms with reproduction and Asian furniture. It doesn't matter where something is from so long as you like it.

Small luxuries such as flowers and candles matter in a bedroom. It's also the room for photographs and souvenirs that bring back nice memories. Have bedroom curtains lined with black-out interlining or install an inexpensive black-out blind. A bedroom is all about cosiness so, while bare windows look well in other rooms, here you'll want a feeling of being cocooned.

Ideally a guest bedroom should be both welcoming and comfortable. It should be interesting without being too strongly personal. If space is available, include a capacious dressing table, which can double as a desk, as well as a comfortable chair and good lighting. Don't forget small but important details like plentiful towels, fresh flowers, recent magazines, water to drink and glasses Remember too an extra throw or blanket in case the nights get chilly. You want your guests to remember your home with pleasure, especially their own private sanctuary.

A higher thread count doesn't mean better-quality bedlinen. A 400-thread-count from a good brand is much better than a 700-thread-count from another. It's all about the quality of cotton the manufacturer uses. Linens that are made in Europe tend to be of top-quality fibre and are therefore very hardwearing. Before buying, look and see where something is made: Indian and Chinese cottons are not good. Always feel the fabric – it should feel cold, smooth and crisp. I've come across 800-thread-count sheets that feel like cardboard because they're made from short-fibre cotton.

bathrooms

If there's one concern shared by those who undertake the renovation of a period house, it is, when it comes to bathrooms, to create a bigger, more luxurious room than the existing one. But finding the space for a large bathroom in such houses isn't easy. Which is why many people merge a small bedroom with an existing bathroom. This is what the owner of this house did to create a large bathroom that connects to the main bedroom, with a freestanding bath.

IN RECENT YEARS the bathroom has come to be described as a 'place to hang out' and the cliché is true. We spend more quality time in the bathroom than ever before. The bathroom is about escape and being alone to coiffe, calm and collect yourself. A bathroom should be restful and relaxing but also functional. Bathroom makeovers don't need to be as difficult as you might imagine. It's possible to make a few small changes, such as adding new taps and sink or doing a paint job or redoing the tiles, that will – without spending a lot of money – give the room a new feeling. First take stock of what you need to do. Think about who will be using the bathroom and how much use it will get. Do you you want to recreate the luxury feel of a spa or have something more simple? And, of course, how much can you afford to spend? There are so many styles, fixtures and materials out there that it helps to have an idea what you want before you start looking and, while staying open to new ideas, stick with your own priorities.

A bathroom should be easy to clean and maintain. Never choose any colour of sanitary ware other than white as colours date quickly. There's nothing wrong with opting for an inexpensive tile – you don't need to go bananas on the latest gimmick – and instead put money into the sink, bath, toilet and shower. In my opinion, bathrooms should be as light, bright and airy as possible. Start by visiting bathroom showrooms to find ideas, then look at your own space and think about what works and what doesn't. Maybe some fittings can be retained and smartened up. Maybe you'd like a separate bath and shower if you've got the space, or perhaps a shower over bath is the only option. If you decide to get serious with a particular showroom, bring them a rough floor plan of the room. Mark the positions of existing plumbing, electrics, radiators, windows and door. In particular, note where the oil stack is (that's the large pipe that carries waste away from the toilet) as moving it will probably be expensive. Not placing sanitary

Above: A bowl sink is a bit of a cliché but still nice. This one is made from resin and mounted on a purpose-built storage unit. Note how the mirror is on the wall to the right, not above the sink – it works just as well but is a little less predictable. Recessing a tap into the wall turns it into a feature. Small luxuries such as flowers and good toiletries make a difference. This is an en-suite bathroom and has a sliding door with frosted glass panel dividing it from the bedroom. A sliding door is a great option if space is tight.

Below: When buying a bath remember that while steel baths are more durable, acrylic ones have a warmer feel and come in a greater variety of shapes. If you want a bath in the centre of your room, it's likely that plumbing will have to be altered and the floor taken up. A large bathroom provides the space to set the bath centre-stage, but a standard bath can be lifted out of the ordinary by a side panel painted a subtle colour contrasting with the rest of the walls. In this Dublin bathroom, the bath-surround has been topped with limestone tiles that create a ledge to sit on. Large baths are wonderful but consider the practicalities. A very deep or wide bath can put a strain on your boiler capacity. Weight could also be a problem. Check with your builder, plumber or bathroom-designer before making a purchase.

Overleaf: Vintage pieces can be reconditioned and have a charm and style that contrasts well with a contemporary setting. Many old styles can look as fresh, timeless and clean today as they did years ago. If you're lucky enough to inherit an original feature or fixture, leave it in place and spruce it up.

ware too close together is key. Meet your builder at the showroom so he can determine if everything you are buying is suitable (for example, a bath could be too heavy for the floor or a shower not suitable for your water pressure). Many showrooms offer a full design and fitting service and it's often best to go this route and hand the job over to them. Yes, they will charge but the better ones won't rip you off and it could be worth saving yourself the hassle of dealing with a third-party builder. Other showrooms simply sell bathroom fittings and devices, leaving the customer to employ an interior designer or to design the room themselves. If you are taking this approach, consult your plumber or builder early on to identify any limitations.

ask yourself:

- Is the bathroom is large enough? Is it possible (and can you afford) to relocate it? Or maybe it would be possible to use some space from an adjoining room to enlarge it?

- Do you really need to gut the space to get what you want? Maybe you can make a few small changes, then pamper the place to create a luxury feel?

- Do you have space for double sinks?

- Do you have a lot of beauty products that need a home? Maybe you could have a unit made or find a vintage piece to hold everything?

- How should you light the room? Close-up lighting around the mirror and ceiling fittings on a dimmer switch?

- What are the technicalities you must consider? Can you move the position of the sink and toilet or are they fixed?

- Is your water pressure adequate for the shower fitting you have your eye on?

Try to include a heated towel-rail in your bathroom. If you are redoing your floor it's very easy to have under-floor heating laid under a stone or tile floor. It makes such a difference to the comfort of the room and can be linked to the regular heating system in the rest of the house.

Left: A free-standing bath with free-standing shower and tap.

Below left: This bathroom in County Clare has a walk-in shower built into a purposefully created recess. White marble is a classic that never dates and is carried through the sink-top. The floor is non-slip stone. Note the lighting on each side of the mirror: two lamps throw even light on to the face for shaving or applying make-up. Traditional is sometimes the best way to go: the simple vanity unit into which the sink is set has been painted a nice soft green.

Below right: Lighting in a bathroom needs to range from soft for bathing to strong for shaving and applying make-up. There are safety standards for lights in a bathroom: they must be operated by a pull cord or a switch outside the room. Always have your bathroom light on a dimmer switch. Candles also provide soft light for a relaxing soak.

Opposite: In this Blackrock (Dublin) bathroom a large sheet of mirror is recessed around tiles above the bath. It visually doubles the size of the room. The framed mirror above the sink is more for use in a hallway or living room, but works as a decorative addition. Using things that weren't made for a bathroom adds interest.

wet rooms

A wet room is a fully waterproofed bathroom without enclosures. The walls of the bathroom form the boundaries of the shower. That means no shower tray and an optional glass panel to partly screen the shower. Water falls across the floor and steam fills the space, giving a steam-room feel to your shower.

If you decide on a wet room the most important things to get right are the details: most importantly, water must flow towards a drain. If this is in the middle of the room, it will require that the sides of the room are built higher than the level of the drain. Creating a leak-proof room is complex too: the structure of the room must be very stable (ground floor is better than first) and waterproofed with a layer of fibreglass or lead.

A wet room is ideal for a small bathroom where enclosing the shower in a separate cubicle would encroach on the space. But a small wet room is not the best place for storage. In larger wet rooms, storage can be fitted well away from the shower. Apart from tiling, various types of stone are popular choices for wet-room cladding but even wood can be used if properly sealed.

Wet rooms are often the best solution if space is tight but it is essential to consult a professional designer before installing one. The space must be tanked (treated with several coats of asphalt or fibreglass applied over a plywood base to create a waterproof membrane) and there has to be enough structural support to bear the weight of these heavy materials. However, it's not overly costly to create a wet room.

durable materials for bathrooms

Stone is very versatile: it can be rustic or refined, traditional or modern, easy- or high-maintenance. The only quality that can be commonly ascribed to all types of stone is variety. Unlike ceramic tiles, stone were not designed by man. The characteristics of each type of stone were 'designed' by nature and formed millennia ago. All we can affect are the shape and size of the tile that is cut from the huge boulders of rock quarried from the earth.

In this Dublin city-centre apartment, dark marble creates a soothing atmosphere when contrasted with light-oak trimmings and recessed strip lighting. Instead of a basin, consider a purpose-built shallow trough. These can be bought in many materials, even polished concrete. Here the trough is black marble to match the walls. Add wall-mounted taps and keep it simple.

After processing, the material ranges from weighty slabs to tiny mosaic. Bathroom walls tend to feature four varieties of 'families' of stone: granite, marble, limestone and slate. Each has a particular aesthetic, so the choice will be based as much on personal likes and dislikes as on any practical reasoning.

Granite is extremely hard-wearing, impervious to water, mottled or flecked in appearance, and available in a wide spectrum of colours, particularly darker shades including black, red, brown and green.

Marble, which is associated with an opulent ambience, is usually veined in appearance. It is porous, so it needs to be sealed. Pure marble is white, but other shades (greys, browns, reds, even black) are also found.

Limestone makes for a calm, soothing, contemporary look. It has a high porosity so needs to be sealed and is generally uniform in appearance, with some slight mottling or fossilisation. It is commonly found in golden, buff and sandy tones but also in white, grey, blue or even chocolate-brown.

Slate works particularly well with rustic or ethnic styles of rooms and is naturally waterproof. It usually has a textured surface and is generally charcoal-grey with blue, purple and green variations.

Make sure you explain to your supplier that the stone you require is for use on walls. Stone is heavy, so your wall-covering needs to be as thin and light as possible. Regular-sized, wall-specific tiles are easier to use than large slabs but even so are best applied by professionals. The whole look of your bathroom will be determined not only by the type of stone you choose and the size and shape of the tile but also by the finish given to the stone. A highly-polished finish suggests opulence and glamour and works well for granite and marble. A matt finish is more subtle and modern, while textured finishes caused by tumbling or natural pitting offer a rawer appearance and will hide splash marks well but may be more difficult to keep clean.

Ordinary vinyl emulsion paint is not recommended for bathroom walls if there is a chance that it will be splashed: stains and watermarks will show. Nor will it be resistant to steam and moist conditions, eventually peeling away or being plagued by mould. For this reason, if you are using paint in a bathroom, make sure it's a specialist paint suited to the purpose. Bathroom-specific paint is usually an acrylic-based eggshell paint or has a latex or plastic content, resulting in a silky sheen that will be easy to wipe dry. Its does not claim to be totally waterproof, though, so don't use it as an alternative to tiles in wet areas.

Polished plaster, also known as Venetian plaster, is a centuries-old wall render that famously adorned Italian palaces and churches. Its smooth glossy look can be sumptuous and decorative, or with texture and pigmentation it can appear rustic and weathered. Polished plaster is particular suited to bathrooms because it is hard-wearing and waterproof. The base, made of lime, cement and marble dust, is given added protection by layers of wax rubbed into the surface. Application should be left to an expert and you can specify different finishes.

small spaces

A COUPLE who had just bought an apartment on Pembroke Road decided to contact Maria MacVeigh after reading an article in *The Irish Times* about the interior designer's own home. They liked her pared-back style and as their Dublin apartment is tiny (a mere 36 sq metres, less than 400 sq ft) they needed advice to make it more liveable-in. Although it was bought as a pied-à-terre, not a full-time residence, they wanted it to be a pleasant space in which to spend a couple of days each week.

'The apartment was very gloomy,' says MacVeigh. 'There was a living room with an alcove kitchen and a tiny bedroom and bathroom. The place had only two small windows.' But because the apartment is on the top floor, it had an attic space, reached by a hatch in the bathroom. When it was opened up, it revealed a skylight. MacVeigh took this feature as her starting point and decided to create a well that allows light to shine into the apartment, rather than just the attic. The position of the skylight created a natural 'line' for the layout. Behind this imaginary line she positioned a kitchen, shower room and entrance lobby. 'The layout was redesigned with all the services pushed back in line with the skylight, making the living room larger and brighter.'

The width of the new section across the back of the apartment was also determined by the width of the shower tray that would sit in the bathroom and by the dimensions of the washer and dryer in the kitchen. 'The area is differentiated by a change in floor material: these areas are floored in granite, the rest of the apartment has ash wood floors.' The light-well has steel steps set into the wall for access to the attic. Sliding or pivoting ash doors play a big part in the transformation of the space. The bedroom, for example, has two sets. One slides open from the entrance lobby; the other opens on the wall that divides the room from the living area. 'When the door between bedroom and living room is open, this allows you to see both

The bedroom in the apartment is divided from the hall by a sliding oak panel. The bars rise to an attic storage space. Because the apartment is on the top floor it was possible to open a well of light from the attic space, lit by a roof window.

windows in the apartment from both rooms, so the daylight is doubled.' It's a simple but ingenious idea that makes the whole apartment seem bigger. Even from the kitchen, there's now a view of the two windows. Another ash door, this time pivoting, separates the entrance hall from the living room. 'This means the living room can be enclosed and be used as a bedroom but there's access to the bathroom from both sleeping spaces.'

A sliding door separates the kitchen from the living area. 'It has two purposes – defining the dining area and hiding away the kitchen if needs be.' There's still a sense of what lies behind this door as it closes only as far as the counter that runs continuously through the kitchen and living space. A timber shelf sits above this and the wall between is tiled. 'The granite counter where the sink is set is narrower than standard, so it looks more like a sideboard than a countertop. It means the line between where the kitchen ends and the living room begins is defined only by the different flooring.' There are other visual tricks at play. The fireplace surround was repositioned so that it sits more to the living room side of the room. 'It makes the chimney look as if it is further into the room than it actually is and brings the focus to that side.'

Storage is always difficult to organise in a small apartment, but because of the attic space and the fact that the apartment was not to be used for full-time living, not a lot was needed. The wardrobe is located in the entrance hall, next to the bedroom, rather than in the room itself. It fits perfectly within the line that MacVeigh drew to house the utilities, kitchen and shower room. In the shower room, a granite washbasin was specially made to fit the space and to create a seamless look, with tiles in the same material. A chrome towel-rail was mounted on the mirror above the sink to save space.

A limited palette works for a small space as it means less confusion for the eye. 'There's one main colour – bone – and three textures of this shade – the wall colour, the spray-paint finish of the furniture, and the 15x15 wall tiles are all different textures.' Perhaps the most successful feature of this apartment is its adaptability. 'It works when all the doors are open and

Above left: A view to the bathroom from the entrance hall.

Above right: A detail of the living area.

Below left: The view into the living area from the entrance lobby.

Below right: A plan and elevation of the space.

Overleaf: The compact kitchen can be closed off from the main living area by a sliding panel.

when everything is closed away. If the owners want to define the dining area more, they just pull the door towards the kitchen. Or to make the living area cosier, they can close the door to the bedroom.'

tips for small spaces

Remove any internal doors you can and replace them with sliding panel doors to make the space seem larger. This works particularly well in apartments where you might not need the same privacy a family would. Extend door openings right to the ceiling, again to create a greater feeling of space. Use one paint colour throughout, with built-in pieces painted a slightly darker shade. This will help a home to seem twice its size. Small spaces need definition, furniture that stands out and makes a room interesting but it's better to do it with small touches such as cushions or trims than with big statements such as rugs or curtains. You can't have everything small and light in colour, or a room just becomes boring. Use blinds rather than curtains. This has the effect of taking the eye 'beyond the room'.

In a small living room, use one decent-sized sofa and a mix of smaller individual chairs. Low built-in presses means you don't have waste wall space as you would with high shelves. They will give you a place to display photographs and other bits and pieces. Use some tall 'floating' bookshelves, with no gable ends; they create a lighter feeling. Use big art: it adds a bit of punch to a room. Avoid chairs with tall backs. They don't necessarily make chairs more comfortable and block off a great deal of a room. Use a bench-style seat with a back along one side of a dining table. Try to find a long narrow glass table. A lot of people choose a table that's too small because they're afraid to clutter a room.

Install kitchen unit doors with press and release mechanisms rather than fussy handles, which also helps to make them 'fade away'. In a bathroom, suspended sanitary ware (without pedestal bases) is better because it makes cleaning easier and lets you see the whole of the floor. Similarly, a platform style bed is good in a small bedroom because you can see a little more of the floor, which helps make the room look bigger.

In the living area the fireplace surround was repositioned so that it sits more to the living-room side of the room. It makes the chimney look further into the room than it actually is and brings the focus to that side.

organising

bookshelves and storage

PUTTING YOUR HOME in order involves everything from the relatively confined task of coordinating the chaos in your wardrobe to reorganising or rethinking each room. A rigidly tidy home, with no clues about the likes and dislikes of its occupants, is a depressing place to be. Conversely, there's nothing as uncomfortable as a home which is chronically untidy. Attractive objects are worth displaying; old newspapers, discarded toys and shoes are not. Consider too the practical aspects of a 'place for everything and everything in its place'. A devil-may-care attitude to possessions usually means that things can't be found when they are wanted. On the other hand, a well-planned storage system means that a book or a scarf can be located with the minimum amount of search and effort.

Families have an incredible number of possessions, some used daily, others kept for sentimental reasons. For the home to work well, possessions need to be controlled so that things on display are visible only because you want them to be seen. If a frantic tidy-up is a must before anyone comes to visit, if opening a cupboard is fraught with hazard, if you have drawers full of pieces of string, redundant pens and cracked china – installing storage to cope with it all can effect a miraculous transformation. Before you hang so much as a shelf, be ruthless about the clutter. Go through the house and throw away everything broken. Get rid of old magazines. Sort through your paperwork. Remember if it's not useful or beautiful or doesn't have a sentimental attachment, you don't need it, a policy which can apply to everything from furniture to clothes. Items in good condition can probably be sold or given to a local charity shop. Children are great hoarders but will

Opposite: This living room has a lot going on visually but is charming rather than cluttered. Simple free-standing bookcases are often the best way to go as they tend to be inexpesive and can, of course, be taken with you if you move. Find one that is as tall as your room can take: books have a way of multiplying.

Overleaf: Architect Sterrin O'Shea designed hatches for storage in the eaves of this attic conversion and lined the end wall with shelves. The hatches are hidden along the birch-veneered panelled walls. Strip lighting is concealed underneath this panelling, illuminating the grey Marmoleum floor.

Left: Set designer Bob Crowley in a room with built-in shelving for books and other objects built around a fireplace. The shelf depths are varied for interest and to accommodate books of different sizes. It's nice to be able to adjust individual shelves but the mechanism can sometimes be ugly: fixed shelves such as these are inflexible but better-looking. One way to make a large run of shelves less intrusive is to paint the woodwork to match the walls.

Below: One approach to deal with the storage of books is to dedicate an entire wall to them. This is a decorative feature in itself and lends a certain atmosphere to a room. Tall shelves can be reached via a ladder sliding along a bar, as in the Rathmines (Dublin) home pictured here.

usually respond to a plea for toys for a hospital. Freed from the bonds of clutter, rooms look larger, brighter and cleaner. There will be a reduction in wear, tear and breakage too. Things last longer when removed from the risk of being trodden on or chewed by the dog.

Wall-mounted shelves are cheap to buy and easy to fit, with a drill, some rawlplugs, a spirit level and a screwdriver. Shelves look best in quantity, especially if they can be fitted into a recess and run from floor to ceiling. Floating (open-ended) shelves are wonderful and look very light but be careful that things don't fall off. The strength of the shelves will only be as good as the fixing method used, so consult a DIY store if in doubt.

Because free-standing bookcases, cupboards and units are not custom-built for the room, space can be wasted. Well-made free-standing storage won't need the support of a wall to stand upright. Some self-assembly furniture tends to sway if unsupported; diagonal bracing will prevent this and the possibility of it being accidentally toppled. Custom-built wardrobes, bookcases and shelving can be designed to fit oddly-shaped or awkward areas which might otherwise be unused. There are many individuals and companies who specialise in this sort of thing.

In a small home, finding space for storage can be difficult. The most important thing is to make the most of the space by adapting storage to suit your needs. If there isn't room for a conventional outward opening-door, fit bi-fold doors on a roller or shutter blinds instead. Narrow shelves can be used in confined spaces and are easier to manage than deep shelving. Storage furniture is as important visually as upholstery, soft furnishings or any component of your home. As well as the obvious function, storage furniture can double as a room divider or be used to hide an unsightly wall or fill in an awkward space. If you plan to use storage as a room divider, leave some shelving areas open to let light filter through to both parts of the room.

Remember small details such as handles. If you are getting something custom-made, consider press-and-release doors or have a ridge added to

If you plan to use storage furniture for display, make sure that shelves are high enough from top to bottom to house your treasures. Choose materials that will enhance the objects on display and show them to best effect. Glass shelves or glass-fronted cupboards provide a good background for china, glass and sculpture. If you fix mirror panels to the walls between the shelves, you will not only enjoy attractive reflections but make the objects on display seem more plentiful. Or you could fit concealed lighting to highlight them.

the top of the door for opening: anything to make the doors as invisible as possible. If a ready-made piece is perfect for your purposes in every other way, see if handles can be replaced. A wall of storage will make provision for a lot of paraphernalia. What you choose boils down to a question of style, taste and pocket, although here, unlike upholstery, expense does not necessarily indicate quality. Some of the German and Italian ready-made built-in units are particularly smooth and luxurious, but cheaper versions can look just as good, if not better, depending on finish and the final arrangement of possessions on shelves.

If you build in your own bookshelves, consider a break-front style: this has cupboards below and a deep shelf at waist height, which could perhaps be used to hold a television or as a desk of some sort. You would get a different feel by installing an armoire or beauty bookcase if you could afford one. These can often be adapted to hide a television. Either piece would be a handsome addition to any room and provide height and a little drama. A good substitute might be one of those Victorian or Edwardian wardrobes that can often be picked up cheaply at auctions because they are too big for most bedrooms. These can be stripped, re-polished, painted, lacquered or mirrored to create something that's both decorative and very useful. Before you decide on a specific piece of storage furniture, as well as taking your budget into account you should ask yourself...

Do you anticipate moving in the near future? If so you may choose movable rather than fixed storage.

Do you want everything stored out of sight or are there objects that you want left out on show? Don't always think in terms of hiding things away. Some hobbies or interests use equipment or materials that are fascinating and these can often lend character to a room if they are left out on display.

Well-organised storage space is essential if you want a neat and reasonably spacious bedroom. The more clothing, shoes, accessories and luggage that can be tucked away the greater the feeling of space you will have.

Above left: Storage doesn't always have to rise high to be effective. Low cupboards double as display areas and are great for small spaces where wall space is valuable. These low units run along an entire wall and have handle-less panel doors painted just a shade darker than the walls.

Below left: Shelving is really the staple form of storage. These elegant bookshelves complement an antique writing desk and contrast nicely with the contemporary chair.

Above near right: In a hall, keep shoes, hats and scarves out of the way. This long, simple unit was custom-made with drawers. The top acts a seat for putting on shoes.

Above far right: This hinged floor-to-ceiling unit holds kitchen bits and pieces and when closed, it is impossible to tell that it's there. It is essentially a wall that opens and reveals storage.

Below right: Interior designer Paul Austen dreamed up this clever unit for a family room. It houses the television and storage behind panels and disguises the radiator, hidden in the bottom part.

The trick is to match the storage to the objects. Storage facilities ideally need to be adapted to each individual, which means that ready-made systems or pieces of furniture are often not the best solution, because they are likely to address a general storage problem rather than your own.

Different styles of clothing require different storage solutions. Long coats and dresses require a considerable amount of full-length hanging space, usually calculated at a maximum height of 5ft 3in (1.6m). T-shirts, jeans, sweaters, shirt, hats and handbags need either many shallow shelves or drawers measuring 1ft by 1ft 10in. Deep shelves tend to result in piles that fall over. Wardrobe depths should be at least 2 ft (60cm) to hold a full-sized coat hanger complete with clothes hanging on it.

Wardrobe heights up to the ceiling are recommended though you think you won't need the space. It's guaranteed that these will soon be filled with bulky, awkward things. Hanging space is often best divided into two: one section above and another below. The access problems associated with having an upper hanging space have been resolved by the introduction of wardrobe lifts; weighed hanging rails that pull down by means of a central rod.

Storage for shoes can be created on sloping pull-out shelves. They can be stored in clear plastic boxes or in their original boxes with a Polaroid taped to the front detailing the footwear treasures. Shoes can also be stored in hanging fabric units.

Free-standing wardrobes can be challenging to integrate because they take up a large amount of space and are rarely designed to work with your particular clothing problems. The obvious alternative is a fitted wardrobe, or a combination of cupboards and wardrobe. Fitted wardrobes should be as discreet s possible: choose a colour that's close to the shade of your walls. If you can have wardrobes over an entire wall. It might also be possible to incorporate shelves and cupboards in a custom-made unit. The design should look neat and streamlined when the doors are closed, yet suit the storage of virtually every possible type of clothing and object. If you

John Redmond created this area in his wife Karen's dressing room. Note the floating shelves used as a method of display. A console table can often make a suitable dressing table.

Take a few choice favourite items and make them into a display. Don't think of this as clutter but as a means of personalising your home. Limit your displays to a few surfaces rather than using too many things in too many places. Remember there's a fine line between keeping a memory and hanging on to all your clothes or jewellery because they are of sentimental value. Transforming treasured items into a display means you can enjoy them every day. Also think about using unusual items for storage and display, such as these old metal cages on the left for shoes.

choose to incorporate drawers or shelves inside built-in units, make them plentiful, shallow and consider fronting them with plastic, glass or cut-out sections for easy recognition. Remember to allow room for garments that are not used every day, such as sports equipment and skiing clothes.

Custom wardrobes are also best for small bedrooms. A wall of fitted storage will make the room look larger and properly planned. This in turn will reduce the need for other furniture.

Also, bear in mind that it is no good storing something that you cannot easily access when you need it. Although it might make sense, say, to put winter or summer clothes away in high cupboards when the season changes, it makes very little sense to use those same high cupboards for things you need regularly.

There are now many companies and shops that specialise in storage, offering ideas ranging from the small but clever (plastic pockets for shoes that hang from a hook) to the large and expensive (complete systems tailor-made to fit your room). But remember always to plan the storage around the objects that need storing, rather than the other way round.

tips for improving your storage

Good storage means looking for clever ways to increase and expand the space you have. It's possible to do this without spending a lot of money.

Create storage spaces with built-in window seats. Conceal the storage under a padded lid. In a bedroom use a window seat for storing blankets, pillows and winter quilts. Build in low storage consisting of drawers along one wall in a bedroom if wardrobe space is limited. Maximise wardrobe space and choose storage drawers, trolleys, crates and stackable boxes. Instead of having a mishmash of boxes under the bed (provided it's not a divan of course), use plastic bins with wheels for easy access in and out. Be sure they have lids to keep the dust out.

Get organised today. It isn't a chore; it allows you to live with what you love.

Think creatively – you may find space where you least expect it and solutions you didn't think existed.

Buy in sets. Matching hangers create more space in your wardrobe; matching sheets and towels will make your organising easier.

Use nice things as storage: if you like the way it looks you're more likely to use it. Think of things like vintage suitcases and hatboxes and old leather in-and-out trays for your home office.

If you haven't used it, worn it or seen it in a year, give it away.

Your mementos probably aren't giving you much pleasure in the attic. Choose a few, frame or display them and enjoy them every day.

Organise your wardrobe daily. In other words, if you take it out, put it back.

Create a place for everything. If something doesn't have a home, it's sure to get lost or damaged, or become clutter.

In the bathroom, space above the toilet cistern can be fitted with slim shelves to hold soaps, candles and other small items. Try bargain shops for sets of small free-standing shelves. Cabinets don't have to be large to be useful: even a narrow wall-mounted cabinet can be a help. Kitchen suppliers can tailor cabinetry to fit any space you have available. Storage spaces can be created inside cavity construction walls. These are a bonus in small bathrooms or kitchens as they're the right depth for bottles, tins and soaps.

Have a look at any area under your stairs. Step the storage shelves or cupboards to take up the whole space. Use modular furniture units or have a specialist wardrobe company come up with a design just for you. Store awkward items such as a sewing machine or computer inside a cupboard with a pull-out shelf. You'll find the material to convert existing cupboard space available from hardware, office or kitchen suppliers.

Consider a large cupboard or armoire in the sitting room. It will allow you to clear away junk in a jiffy.

home offices

Whether you're working full-time out of your home, or it's for occasional personal use, you'll probably spend quite a few hours in your home office. That's why it's important to ask yourself some questions before you begin decorating, to make sure this space will truly fulfil your needs.

Do you want a relaxing environment or do you need your workspace to be more stimulating?

Will you be having visitors to your office?

Should the look of your office fit in with the rest of your home?

Don't be overwhelmed by overflowing cupboards. Look to shops and catalogues filled with the stuff that organising dreams are made of. Fit out your home with orderly options and storage solutions you will improve your life.

Above (left): In a bedroom, tall chests of drawer are often the most practical solution and, unlike wardrobes, they can be more of a feature piece. Colour-code the clothing inside: not only is it easier to find what you're looking for but it's a great system for keeping things neat.

Above (right): Shoes get dusty at the bottom of a wardrobe: buy clear containers to hold them.

Below: Treat yourself to heavy wood hangers to help your clothes keep their shape and even save you some ironing. Keep cotton-covered hangers for delicate items. Vertical hangers for shirts and trousers are another way to save valuable wardrobe space.

Whatever you decide, your office should be a place where you will enjoy working. First choose the wall colour that will best suit your needs. If you are easily distracted, you may need to surround yourself with soft, muted colours to relax and calm you, and help you get down to work. If you find motivation difficult, you may want to surround yourself with brighter colours to provide you with more energy.

An office has become an essential in many homes. The guest room may be replaced by a work-at-home spot, and it's important that all the elements contribute to a productive time. There are lots of ways to create a good space for working at home without spending a fortune.

If you're lucky enough to have a separate room the task won't be so hard. The key to a good home office is to make use of whatever space you have, whether it's a landing, a small closet, a spare room or a corner of the living room. For greatest efficiency, find a space that can be dedicated to a home-office area. You'll be able to work more professionally if you don't have to move papers off your desk to do something else.

It might be tempting just to move pieces of furniture around until the space works. But if you spend some time actually measuring your space (small as it might be), creating a floor plan, measuring your furniture and thinking it through, the final result will be much more satisfactory.

If you can do any of the work yourself it will save you money. Your home-office space is probably not going to be too big, so consider painting the walls yourself. Can you move furniture or accessories from one part of the house to your new home office? If you don't have to buy some pieces, you'll save a lot. Is there a comfortable chair in the guest room? Do you have some pictures tucked away that would be inspiring and decorative on the walls of your workspace?

Think of other ways you can use inexpensive materials to create shelves, filing systems, in-and-out boxes. Use a decorative flowerpot to hold pencils and scissors. Buy several multi-level shoe-shelves to put on top of the desk

Awkward corners sometimes make perfect office spaces. Go vertical and use every inch of height you have: install shelves to the ceiling and above windows, keeping files easily accessible. This office is in a nook off a kitchen, so the owner can keep on top of paperwork and family meals at the same time.

to hold a printer, paper or books. You'd be amazed what you can find at charity shops, junk shops and auctions. It seems that people are always getting rid of bookshelves and desks and you might find just what you need. Clean off the pieces, sand them down and paint them all the same colour. It will look as though you bought them to match. If you don't want hand-me-downs, keep your eye open for furniture sales or check web sources.

Consider swapping pieces of furniture with a friend. If you have a dining table that doesn't fit in your home, how about exchanging it for a desk you need? Or do you have children's furniture that a neighbour could use in exchange for bookshelves? If you're working full-time at home, be sure to include adequate lighting, music and comfortable seating. Bring in plants and inspiring artwork. After all, you might be spending a lot of time in this new home office.

a garage conversion (overleaf)

Interior designer Philippa Buckley created one of the best garage con-versions I've ever seen. The garage opens off her kitchen and now acts as a laundry room, utility room, storage space and home office. It's not a complicated design but works for her family. The walls are lined with painted MDF units that she designed and had made by a joiner. The doors are smartened by long metal handles. Behind some are a multitude of special shelves and fittings to hold shoes and coats. Another pair of doors opens to reveal a sink. Others hide the washing machine and dryer. Yet another has a pull-out desk for dealing with household paperwork. The floor is perforated metal, the kind you see on trucks, so bicycles can be wheeled through to the rear garden. One important aspect is the lighting: Philippa installed proper recessed lights that provide sufficient illumination for the various tasks carried on here and make it feel like a real room.

Opposite: In home offices, off-whites and cool colours don't distract or disturb, making them a perfect choice. A pale room helps to quiet the nerves, lift the spirits and soothe the soul. Psychologically, these types of colours are calming and meditative, conducive to concentration.

Overleaf: Interior designer Philippa Buckley in the garage she converted to a utility/storage room.

resources

Below are a few random but useful contacts:

Adams (auction house: www.adamsblackrock.com)

Aiden Cavey Interiors (traditional and contemporary furniture: www.cavey.ie)

Alan Gallagher (creative joiner and furniture maker: 087-2265362)

Alan Ward (independent stone dealer: 087-6308078)

Alliance Property Maintenance (household maintenance: www.alliancemaintenance.ie)

Amber Coast (super reliable kitchen and storage joinery: 087-2245364)

Angela O'Connor (interior decorator: www.oconnordesignpartners.com)

Antica (rare stone specialists and cutting edge bathrooms: www.antica.ie)

Architectural Salvage (www.architecturalsalvage.ie)

Architectural World (unusual doors: www.architecturalworld.ie)

Architectural Textiles (textured wall-coverings: email: design@graniamurray.com)

Arcon Bathrooms (great service and sanitary ware: www.arconbathrooms.com)

Arena Kitchens & Bathrooms (up to the minute: www.arenakitchens.com)

Arnotts (www.arnotts.ie)

Artefaction (specialists in stone flooring and fireplaces: www.artefaction.ie)

Audrey Adams (furniture restorer used by Francis Street dealers: 01-6771960)

Avoca (www.avoca.ie)

Bellissima, County Cork (contemporary furniture: www.bellissima.ie)

Bill Simpson (interior designer: billsimpson@eircom.net)

Blue Door (colourful Swedish tablewear and accessories: www.thebluedoordirect.ie)

Bo-Concept (affordable Danish contemporary furniture: www.boconcept.com)

Bottom Drawer (luxury items for bed and bath: 01-6056696)

Brendan Gallagher (County Waterford kitchen-maker: 086-2641547)

Brian Leach Construction (top-class builder: 01-6244520)

Brian S. Nolan (fabrics: www.briansnolan.ie)

Brown Thomas (bountiful accessories and chic furniture: www.brownthomas.ie)

Buckley's Auction House (01-2844717)

Carpe Diem, County Kerry (quirky contemporary furniture: 064-36490)

Caxton Prints (17th- and 18th-century prints: 01-4530060)

Ceadogan Rugs, County Wexford (bespoke handmade rugs: www.ceadogan.ie)

Chester Beatty Library Gift Shop (ethnic accessories: 01-4070750)

Christopher O'Neill & Sons Marble Works (fireplace restoration: 01-2955910).

Clancy Chandeliers (period lighting and restoration: www.clancychandeliers.com)

Colin Dunne (excellent kitchen- and wardrobe-maker: 01-2810897)

Costello Flowers (brilliant florist: 01-2841864)

Cremins Moiselle, County Wicklow (fabrics to the trade but worth a visit: www.creminsmoiselle.ie)

Damien Clarke (perfectionist window cleaner: 086-3331913)

David Skinner Wallpaper (handmade wallpaper: www.skinnerwallpaper.com)

Declan O'Loughlin (vinyl flooring: www.polyflor.com)

Décor (rustic Asian furniture: 01-4759010)

Dennis Drumm (auction house: 01-8452819)

Design Classic Direct (classic 20th-century furniture reproductions: www.designclassicsdirect.ie)

Design House (Porsche kitchens and others: www.designhouseconcepts.ie)

Designer Spray (specialists in repainting and rejuvenating kitchen cabinets: 01-4922559)

Design-flow (office furniture: www.designflow.ie)

D-Light (inspiring lighting designer and suppy: e-mail info@dlight.ie)

Domino Design, County Wicklow (bespoke kitchens and bedroom furniture: www.dominodesign.ie)

Drawing Room (traditional lighting and accessories: 01-6772083)

Drumm Antiques, County Wexford (antique French furniture with character: www.drumantiques.com)

Dry Zone (alternative heating systems: www.dryzone.ie)

Duff Tisdall (naturally low-key contemporary furniture: www.duff-tisdall.ie)

Dunnes Home (www.dunnesstores.com)

E.V. Kidd (smartens wood floors by sanding, staining, removing scratches: 01-8110722)

Eden Home & Garden (American-style contemporary furniture: 01-7642004)

Elegant John (bathroom fittings: www.elegantjohn.ie)

Esther Sexton Antiques (01-4730909)

Evy Richard (picture hanging service: artevy@dublin.ie)

Fassbinder & English (glamorous painted furniture and finishes: www.fassbinderenglish.com)

Fired Earth (best for tiles and traditional bathrooms: www.firedearth.co.uk)

Fitzmawn Interiors & Tiles (unusual sanitary ware: www.fitzmawninteriors.ie)

Foxford Woollen Mills, County Mayo (upholstered furniture and strong fabrics: www.foxfordwoollenmills.ie)

Frank Delaney (good upholsterer: 087-6370693)

Frank Kierse (specialist in cleaning Marmoleum floors: 01-2808605)

French Country Interiors, County Tipperary (French art-deco style furniture: www.frenchcountryinteriors.ie)

Gallery 29 (vintage prints: www.gallery29.ie)

Garuda Design, Belfast (high-end furniture and design: www.garudadesign.com)

Gary Thornton (picture-framer: 086-2416943)

George Stackpoole Antiques, County Limerick (061-396409)

Gerflor (rubber flooring: gerflorirl@gerflor.com)

Glass Centre (for mirror etc: 01-4541711)

Greg Knapik (wood floor sanding and staining: 087-2160503)

Gregory Curran (interior designer: gcurran@gcurrandesign.com)

H&F Enterprises, County Tipperary (specialists in re-enamelling stoves: www.handfenterprises.ie)

Harriet's House (lush furniture and lighting: www.harrietshouse.ie)

Herman Wilkinson (auctions: 01-4972245)

Hilda O'Connor Interiors (rich furniture and fabrics: www.hocinteriors.com)

Holland's, County Cork (quality but affordable oriental rugs: www.hollands.ie)

Houseworks (furniture and kitchens: www.houseworks.ie)

Howards Storage World (storage devices: www.howardsstorageworld.com)

Hunter Dunn, County West Meath (cosy warm furniture: www.hunterdunn.ie)

Ideal Bathrooms (bathrooms: www.idealbathrooms.com)

Ideal Standard (bathrooms: www.idealstandard.ie)

Ikea, Belfast (www.ikea.co.uk)

Imagine Wallpaper, County Kilkenny (bespoke photographic wallpaper: www.imaginewallpaper.com)

In-House at the Panelling Centre (storage, kitchen and bedrooms: www.in-house.ie)

Inreda (low-key cutting-edge contemporary furniture: www.inreda.ie)

Interior Image (affordable contemporary furniture, fabrics and flooring: www.interiorimage.ie)

Jacinta McCarthy (specialist in touching up and repairing stone floors: 087-2339324)

Jane Williams (guilder: 087-7819965)

Jennifer Goh (Asian furniture: www.jennifergohdesign.co)

Jim Lawlor (architect: e-mail: office@meltedsnow.net)

John Farrington (gilt mirrors: 01-6791899)

John McCarthy of Brooks Thomas (wood and under-floor heating: 01-2940200)

Julie Dillon (skilled curtain-maker: 087-9694142)

K2 Stone (stone specialists: www.k2stone.ie)

Kayfoam Woolfson (the most comfortable beds: www.kayfoamwoolfson.com)

Kehoe Interiors (affordable painted kitchens and furniture: www.kehoeinteriors.ie)

Liam Slattery (picture-framer: 01-4978446)

Limited Edition (bright and wacky furniture: www.limitededition.ie)

Living Quarters (simple but quality bedroom furniture: www.livingquarters.ie)

Living, County Wicklow (contemporary furniture: www.living.ie)

Lomi (high-end contemporary furniture: www.lomi.ie)

Lost Weekend, County Wexford (select contemporary furniture from brilliant designers: www.lostweekend.ie)

Mac's Salvage Warehouse (01-6792110)

Maison, County Meath (pretty furniture and fabrics: 046-9066226)

Margaret Buggy, County Carlow (curtain-maker extraordinaire: 059-9159981)

Martsworth Carpets, County Wicklow (0404-40113)

Mary Wrynne (amazing curtain-maker:www.marywrynne.ie)

McNally Living (contemporary furniture and kitchens: www.mcnallyliving.ie)

Meadows & Byrne (www.meadowsandbyrne.com)

Mealy's, County Kilkenny (auctions: 056-4441229)

Michael O'Connell Antiques (www.connellantiques.com)

Miele (appliances: www.miele.ie)

Mimosa Interiors (pale and painted or dark and sexy mix of traditional and contemporary: 01-2602443)

Minima (best of the best international contemporary furniture: www.minima.ie)

Mobilia (contemporary furniture: www.mobilia.ie)

Montana furniture (contemporary bedroom furniture: www.montana.ie)

Mount Leinster Stone, County Carlow (www.mountleinsterstone.ie)

MRCB Paints (www.mrcb.ie)

Murphy Sheehy (fabrics: www.murphysheehy.com)

National Lighting Showroom (www.nationallighting.ie)

New England Designs (New England-style furniture):www.newenglanddesigns.eu)

Niall Mullen (art-deco furniture: www.niallmullen antiques.com)

Niamh Barry (bespoke lighting designer: www.niamhbarrydesign.com)

No. 6 (Foxford furniture and accessories by Helen McAlinden: 01-6708846)

O'Driscoll Furniture (contemporary Irish furniture: www.oddesign.ie)

O'Sullivan Antiques (www.osullivanantiques.com)

Octopus Cleaning (house-cleaning service: 086-8312957)

Oriental Rug Company (affordable rugs: www.orientalrugs.ie)

Orior, County Down (contemporary furniture made to order: www.oriorbydesign.com)

Oven Clean (ovenclean.ie)

Oxfam Home (01-4020555)

Peter Johnson Interiors (unusual, one-off furniture, lighting and objects: www.peterjohnsoninteriors.ie)

Pia Bang Home (www.piabanghome.ie)

Plush Interiors. County Sligo (good for sofas and armchairs: 071-9154912)

Porter & Ryle, County Wicklow (high-quality fabrics, wallpapers and paints: www.porterryle.com)

Quest Home & Garden (painted furniture: www.questinteriors.ie)

Retrospect (vintage furniture: www.retrospect.ie)

Robbie Keating (specialist painter: 087-6424166)

Roberts Furniture (upolsterers: 01-8256250)

Roche Bobois (high-quality contemporary furniture from France: www.rochebobois.com)

Roisin Cross Silks (fabrics: www.silks.ie)

Rug Art (contemporary rugs: www.rugart.ie)

Sarah Cruise (interior designer: info@designintervention.ie)

Scotts (wood flooring: www.scotts.ie)

Scudding Clouds (interior design and Japanese plaster specialists: www.scuddingclouds.ie)

Shaker Store, County Kildare (Shaker furniture: www.shakerstore.ie)

Shutters of Ireland (www.shuttersofireland.com)

Silk Road Interiors (Asian furniture and fabrics: 01-8485044)

Sirin Lewendon (interior designer: sirin@sirinlewendon.com)

Snaidero (Italian kitchens: www.italiandesign.ie)

Spendlove Kitchens (contemporary kitchens: www.spendlovefurniture.com)

Storage Solutions (storage devices and shelving: www.storagesolutions.ie)

Surreal Designs, County Galway (contemporary kitchens: www.surrealdesigns.ie)

TC Mathews Carpets (01-4503822)

Tilestyle (bathrooms and tiles: www.tilestyle.ie)

Tommy Doyle Cabinetmakers (furniture makers: 01-4013059)

Tommy O'Reilly (reliable and creative builder: toreilly@sunlight.ie)

Town & Country, County Cork (country-look furniture, fabrics and carpets: 021-4501468)

Tru Curve (specialists in curved glass: 01-4730710)

Versatile Bathrooms, County Meath (www.versatile.ie)

Victorian Salvage & Joinery Company (01-6727000)

Watsham & Bohn (furniture and design: www.watshambohn.com)

White Sands (specialists in eco-friendly decoration and non-toxic paint: www.whitesandsdesigns.com)

Wild Child Originals (vintage furniture: www.wildchildoriginals.com)

William Free (specialists in contemporary carpets: 01-6684763).

Willie Duggan Lighting, County Kilkenny (one of best lighting suppliers: www.williedugganlighting.com)

World Design (ethnic accessories from Africa: www.worlddesign.ie)

acknowledgements

Thank you to *The Irish Times*, *Image Interiors*, *The Gloss* and *Living Etc* for very kind assistance with photography. Thank you also to architects and designers Grania Murray (www.graniamurray.com; Maria MacVeigh (www.mariamacveigh.com); Sterrin O'Shea (www.sosa.com); Deirdre Danaher (ddanaher@eircom.net); Philippa Buckley (www.studio44.ie); Dave O'Shea (www.odosarchitects.com); Helen Roden and Joseph Ensko (www.merrionsquareinteriors.com); Milo Fitzgerald (milofitz@eircom.net) and Paul Austen (paulausten.design@gmail.com). Many thanks to those who allowed their homes be featured in this book, including Liz Nilsson (www.liznilsson.com); Sarah Gill (www.seagreen.ie); Helen Kilmartin (www.minima.ie); Monique McQuaid (www.gastromonique.com); John Barrett (www.johnbarrett.com); Olivia Morris (www.oliviamorrisshoes.com); Samantha Treacy (www.samanthatreacy.com); Ryan McElhinney (www.ryanmcelhinney.com); Bob Crowley; Hilary and Philip Fox-Mills; John and Karen Redmond; Sonia Reynolds and Barry Lyons. Grateful thanks also to those who worked on this book – Jo O'Donoghue of Currach Press, Richard Parfrey, Sinead McKenna and Frances O'Rourke.

photography credits

Front cover photograph by Tim Young; author photos on back cover flap and page 7 by Bryan O'Brien; page 5 by David Sleator; page 8 by Paul Massey; page 12 by James Fennell; page 16 by David Sleator; page 21 top left by Lois Crighton, others by Tim Young; page 23 by Tim Young; page 24 by Paul Massey; page 26-7 by Paul Massey; page 28 by John Phelan; page 30 by Barry McCall; page 32 by David Sleator; page 34 by Lois Crighton; page 35 by John Phelan; page 37 by Barry McCall; page 39 by Paul Massey; page 40 (top) by Luke White, (bottom) by Paul Massey; page 42 by Marie Louise Halpenny; page 44 by John Phelan; page 49 by Tim Young; page 50 by Graham Atkins Hughes; page 55 by Lois Crighton; page 56 by Paul Massey; page 58 by Tim Young; page 60-1 by James Fennel; page 62-3 by Verity Welstead; page 70 by Graham Atkins Hughes; page 72-3 by John Phelan; page 74 by Lois Crighton; page 77 by Paul Massey; page 81 by Tim Young; page 85-6 by Lois Crighton; page 90 by Marie Louise Halpenny; page 96-7 by Verity Welstead; page 121 by Lois Crighton; pages 124-31 by Veronica Escudero; page 132 by Tim Young; page 134-5 by Marie Louise Halpenny; page 139 by Barry McCall; page 140 (top) by Lois Crighton, (bottom) by Barry McCall; page 143 by Graham Atkins Hughes; page 147 (top left) by Barry McCall, (bottom left) by Lois Crighton; page 147-8 by James Fennell; page 150 by Paul Massey; page 153-4 by Bryan O'Brien. Photographer Lois Crighton can be contacted at www.loiscrighton.com; Tim Young at www.timyoung.co.uk; James Fennell at www.jamesfennell.com; Paul Massey at www.paulmasseyphotography.com; David Sleator at dsleator@irish-times.ie; Barry McCall at www.mccallstudio.com; Marie Louise Halpenny at www.marielouisehalpenny.com; Gaham Atkin Hughes at www.grahamatkinshughes.com; Veronica Escudero at www.veronicae.com; Bryan O'Brien at bobrien@irish-times.ie